4553 859

P9-DNX-943

BARNES & NOBLE® READER'S COMPANION™

The
Corrections

WITHDRAWN

BARNES & NOBLE® READER'S COMPANION™
Today's take on tomorrow's classics.

FICTION
THE CORRECTIONS by Jonathan Franzen
I KNOW WHY THE CAGED BIRD SINGS by Maya Angelou
THE JOY LUCK CLUB by Amy Tan
THE LOVELY BONES by Alice Sebold
THE POISONWOOD BIBLE by Barbara Kingsolver
THE RED TENT by Anita Diamant
WE WERE THE MULVANEYS by Joyce Carol Oates
WHITE TEETH by Zadie Smith

NONFICTION
THE ART OF WAR by Sun Tzu
A BRIEF HISTORY OF TIME by Stephen Hawking
GUNS, GERMS, AND STEEL by Jared Diamond
JOHN ADAMS by David McCullough

JONATHAN FRANZEN'S

The
Corrections

BARNES & NOBLE
BOOKS

EDITORIAL DIRECTOR Justin Kestler
EXECUTIVE EDITOR Ben Florman
DIRECTOR OF TECHNOLOGY Tammy Hepps

SERIES EDITOR John Crowther
MANAGING EDITOR Vincent Janoski

WRITER Laban Carrick Hill
EDITOR Matt Blanchard
DESIGN Dan O. Williams

This edition published by Spark Publishing

Spark Publishing
A Division of SparkNotes LLC
120 Fifth Avenue, 8th Floor
New York, NY 10011

ISBN 1-58663-861-0

Library of Congress Cataloging-in-Publication Data available upon request

Printed and bound in the United States

Contents

A TOUR OF THE NOVEL an overview of the book **1**

Home for the Holidays *The Corrections* ditches mistletoe and yuletide cheer for Baltic mobsters, talking turds, and drug-smuggling housewives.

JOURNEYS the characters and their stories **21**

The Corrections We Make Franzen shows us how each of our lives is a series of corrections—our attempts to correct the faults of our parents and the mistakes of our pasts.

POINTS OF VIEW a conversation about *The Corrections* **31**

Bringing It All Back Home Looking past the media storm, what do readers of *The Corrections* really think about the novel?

A WRITER'S LIFE Jonathan Franzen's story **49**

Resurrecting the Great Novel Franzen worked his way into the heart of the American literary scene with his fiction, his essays, and his stated goal of writing the next Great American Novel.

THE WORLD OUTSIDE the Lamberts' 1990s America **53**

Keeping Up With the Lamberts From St. Jude to Manhattan, Lithuania to a cruise ship, Franzen's characters can't escape the great American rat race.

A BRIEF HISTORY the critics respond to *The Corrections* **57**

The Oprah Wars *The Corrections* brought Franzen fame and fortune—and a ten-round grudge match with the most powerful woman in media.

EXPLORE books to consider reading next **61**

Other Books of Interest In writing *The Corrections* and his earlier novels, Franzen has turned to a number of American literary giants for inspiration.

BARNES & NOBLE® READER'S COMPANION™

WITH INTELLIGENT CONVERSATION AND ENGAGING
commentary from a variety of perspectives, BARNES
& NOBLE READER'S COMPANIONS are the perfect
complement to today's most widely read and
discussed books.

○　○　○

Whether you're reading on your own or as part of a
book club, BARNES & NOBLE READER'S COMPANIONS
provide insights and perspectives on today's most
interesting reads: What are other people saying about
this book? What's the author trying to tell me?

○　○　○

Pick up the BARNES & NOBLE READER'S COMPANION
to learn more about what you're reading. From the
big picture down to the details, you'll get today's take
on tomorrow's classics.

BARNES & NOBLE® READER'S COMPANION™

The
Corrections

Home for the Holidays

The Corrections ditches mistletoe and yuletide cheer for Baltic mobsters, talking turds, and drug-smuggling housewives.

○ ○ ○

AT HEART, JONATHAN FRANZEN'S *The Corrections* is a holiday fable gone terribly awry. The classic tale of redemption during the Christmas holidays that we've come to cherish in novels like *A Christmas Carol* and movies like *Miracle on 34th Street* is stillborn in *The Corrections.* The characters, who desperately want to find peace—not only peace on earth, but peace of mind—are imprisoned in a consumer culture that values only things. If it's not tangible and can't be quantified, then it doesn't exist—and if it doesn't exist, it can't be owned and, consequently, experienced. In this culture that holds a person's latest achievement and latest bank statement as the only currencies of respect, traditional notions like the Christmas spirit are perceived as hopelessly outdated.

The Corrections introduces us to the Lamberts, a typical post-World War II baby-boom family consisting of a father, mother, and three grown children. Enid, the mother, dreams of gathering her family together for one last Christmas at home. All she wants is for her three grown children to return to St. Jude, Indiana, and spend Christmas like the family they once were. The only problem is getting everyone there.

Enid isn't the only one with problems. Her husband, Alfred, is quickly degenerating due to Parkinson's disease, and it's not clear whether he'll even recognize his family come Christmas. The Lamberts' oldest son, Gary, is a successful bank executive in Philadelphia, but he faces a wife and sons who hate his parents and refuse to travel to St. Jude. On top of this, he's in the throes of a midlife crisis that has sent him spiraling into depression. The middle son, Chip, was recently fired from his position as an English professor at a New England college. Now out of a job, he has signed on as an assistant to a Baltic mobster and is caught in the middle of a coup in Lithuania. The youngest and only daughter, Denise, is a chef, a rising star in the restaurant world. But her personal life is in shambles after she has affairs not only with her boss, but her boss's wife as well.

If all the Lamberts can free themselves from problems of their own making, then Enid's Christmas dream will come true. As the plot unfolds, each family member confronts the fact that he or she hasn't attained the American dream. This realization prompts each character to make a "correction," in much the same way that the stock market makes a correction when economic expectations are overly optimistic.

The Corrections achieves a unique and monumental feat for a novel of the twenty-first century—it reinvents the classic genre of tragic realism that dominated fiction a century ago. In the nineteenth and early twentieth centuries, Harriet Beecher Stowe's *Uncle Tom's Cabin*, Upton Sinclair's *The Jungle*, and other "big issue" novels exposed the shocking and lurid reality of the underclass for middle-class readers. *Uncle Tom's Cabin* brought the reader into the unknown and unseen life of slaves in order to create a story that indicted slavery. *The Jungle* did the same for the Chicago stockyards, where thousands of meatpacking workers toiled in horrible and unsanitary conditions each day. Not only did Sinclair create sympathy for the exploited and poorly treated immigrant workers in the meatpacking industry, he also aroused widespread public concern about food safety and quality, which helped bring about the passage of federal food inspection laws. Sinclair somewhat ironically remarked, "I aimed at the public's heart and by accident hit it in the stomach."

These novels of tragic realism exposed worlds hidden from literate Americans who lived relatively comfortable lives on the better side of town. They offered a safe way for readers to learn the truth and gave these readers an outlet for feelings of outrage and righteousness—without soiling their clothes. These stories were chock-full of repulsive acts and sordid details, giving them the feeling of truth readers hungered for. Consequently, readers who were attracted to the lurid scenarios of the books were happy never to experience the reality of lower-class life firsthand.

The Corrections serves up a similarly grim American realism with a refreshing dollop of humor. Franzen turns the genre on its ear by suggesting that the homes and backyards of the well-educated classes harbor social ills just as severe and widespread as those the lower classes face. The result is that the voyeuristic literate population can no longer say, "There, but for the grace of God, go I." Instead, readers must confront the reality of the pared-down statement "There go I." In such a way, *The Corrections* portrays the painful consequences of a family that bought wholly into the post–World War II American dream: the midlevel executive husband, the homemaker wife, and three children (slightly better than an underachieving 2.5 children). While Stowe and Sinclair portray the lives of desperately poor people, Franzen turns the tables by suggesting that the lives of "successful" Americans are equally as diminished as the suffering masses of a century ago.

Interestingly, Franzen resists wrapping up *The Corrections* into a neat package of righteous moral outrage like Stowe and Sinclair. He neither endorses nor disparages his characters' actions or his society's values. The moral of Franzen's story is something much like the conclusion of Samuel Beckett's existentialist novel

> The **characters move on** after a **series** of **minor epiphanies— corrections** —without the **benefit** of any **real redemption.**

The Unnamable: "[Y]ou must go on, I can't go on, I'll go on." By the end of *The Corrections*, the characters move on after a series of minor epiphanies—corrections—without the benefit of any real redemption.

Gitanas Misevicius, the book's disgraced Lithuanian deputy prime minister and criminal warlord, sums up the novel when (quoting Marx) he describes the situation in Lithuania as a "tragedy rewritten as a farce." For us, this statement is key to understanding and appreciating *The Corrections*. The story might appear to be an American tragedy, but in the face of the twentieth century's monumental atrocities—the Holocaust, Stalin's purges, the Cambodian genocide, and others, tragedy on this small scale can only reach the level of farce. Franzen, aware of this, takes us on a hilarious roller coaster ride through contemporary middle-class American culture. Not to laugh at the pale desperation these characters inhabit is to give up hope—and that would be the real tragedy.

ST. JUDE

Meet the Lamberts—Enid and Alfred. They're a retired couple whose suburban home has become a prison. Enid is a homemaker whose children have grown up and left, so she no longer has a home to make. Alfred is the classic man in the gray flannel suit, a former engineer for the Midland Pacific Railroad. After retiring, Alfred hasn't found another role to play, so he sits in his oversized leather chair in the basement as if he were just one of the things stored down there.

The novel opens to "[t]he madness of an autumn prairie cold front." This ominous image of an impending winter sets the stage. The trees are bare, and the children's bedrooms have been empty for years. To describe this environment, Franzen chooses an oddly abstract and cold word, "gerontocratic," which means "controlled by a governing group of elders." Rather than "retirement community," which has a neutral, almost positive feel, Franzen chooses gerontocratic—a word that describes the suburban community of St. Jude (where almost everyone is retired) and also hints at the ironic distance at which the narrator keeps himself from this story.

The hollowness of this opening description sets the stage for the first scene of *The Corrections.* Alfred is in the basement of their home, feeling a vague sense of danger. Things are no longer right in this house that was built to raise a family and harbor the bright sounds of growing children. The wicker chair that took Alfred a mere hour to paint a decade earlier has taken him weeks to paint now, and he's not even close to finishing. He passes time dozing in his leather chair like a passenger awaiting the arrival of a train or a plane. Franzen describes Alfred's state by explaining how out of control things are in the household. A colony of crickets has taken over the basement. Alfred, for whatever reason, urinates in empty Yuban coffee cans and hides them under his workbench, even though there's a bathroom just a few steps away. When Alfred tries to take control of the family finances, he can't manage even the simplest calculations.

Yet this is a man who spent his life managing thousands of miles of railroad track. Life has gone sadly—but hilariously—awry.

Upstairs, Enid is frantic, unable to manage an empty house. Just years before, she was able to keep order easily, even with three children and a husband messing up the place. Now Enid has to take shortcuts to maintain the high standards of order that she and Alfred have come to expect. She hides the mail because she can't seem to manage the several pounds that arrive each week. She stuffs unopened envelopes into the back of drawers, under furniture, and behind boxes in closets—anywhere out of sight. She can't make sense of the mail she does open, including a health insurance bill for twenty-two cents. One letter threatens legal action if the bill goes unpaid, but another informs her to ignore any bills for less than twenty-five cents. The world no longer seems to add up the way it used to. A dutiful housewife intent on saving every penny, Enid compulsively clips coupons for things she will never buy. Long after the coupons

"Ringing throughout the house was an alarm bell that no one but Alfred and Enid could hear directly. It was the alarm bell of anxiety."

have expired, she stores them in drawers around the house, content with the knowledge that they're there, just in case.

Amid this anxiety for order, Enid has misplaced an important letter from the Axon Corporation. We're not told why this letter is important, only that Enid wants to keep it from Alfred. While she frantically searches the house, she encounters Alfred in their bedroom upstairs, packing for a vacation that doesn't begin for a few more days. By now, it's clear that Alfred isn't simply old and forgetful, but that there's clearly something wrong with him—though we still don't exactly know what.

The key moment in this section of the novel comes when Enid, seeing Alfred packing, asks him what he's doing. Alfred tries to muster the faculties to respond with a simple, declarative sentence, but the effort is nearly beyond him. Franzen depicts this struggle with magnificently lyrical and remarkably constructed sentences. The sentence encompasses nearly an entire page and contains countless clauses, all just trying to arrive at a statement with a subject, predicate, and object. In terms of sheer length, the sentence is reminiscent of the snaking, page-long sentences that appear in novelist Henry James's later works. James's sentences are meant to contain the chaotic emotions and thoughts of his characters; Franzen's sentences illustrate just how close Alfred is to spiraling out of control.

By the end of "St. Jude," the Lambert household appears to be on its last legs, like a heart in dire need of a pacemaker. The emotional and physical muscles of the home have deteriorated to near immobility. Enid, however, is determined to bring her life back from the dead, to do conventional family things, like going on a cruise or orchestrating a Christmas gathering. The conflict between Enid's Christmas fantasy and the true state of things in the household creates immense potential for comedy. *The Corrections* is poised to exploit these differences to create a biting satire on the gap between expectations and reality.

> The Lambert household is on its last legs, like a heart in dire need of a pacemaker.

THE FAILURE

Now that we know Enid and Alfred, Franzen introduces their children—Gary, Chip, and Denise. To emphasize this family's ideal structure—so he can tear it down later—Franzen patterns the children after a classic 1960s family profile developed by psychologist Alfred Adler. In his model, Adler identified certain birth-order patterns in families of that era. He argued that each child in a family played a certain role depending on whether he or she was born first, second, or last.

In Adler's system, the oldest child is effectively dethroned by the next child born. He has to learn to share. His parents have high expectations for him: they give him extra responsibility and expect him to set an example. In *The Corrections*, Gary is the oldest of the Lambert children. A successful businessman like his father and himself a father to three sons, Gary excels at winning his parents' approval.

Adler believes the second child often feels "sandwiched in" between the other two children. As a result, he may feel squeezed out of a position of privilege and significance. This child often becomes the rebel in the family and has difficulty finding his place—not just in the family, but in the world as a whole. Chip, the middle Lambert child, is clearly the radical in the family. He doesn't conform to the expectations of anyone, especially his parents.

The last child grows up with many people in the role of mother and father. She feels pressure to stand out from the others. Often, she has huge plans. But she's also the one who tries to keep the family together. Denise more or less fits this profile: she's the star chef at a hot restaurant, but she never forgets her family. She works harder than her two brothers to realize her mother's wishes for Christmas.

We first meet Chip as he picks up his parents at LaGuardia Airport. He is the most overtly outrageous of the Lambert siblings—he is thirty-eight years old but seemingly has the maturity of a teenager. He's obsessed with sex, dresses in hipster leather and ear studs, and can barely tolerate appearing in public with his parents. Before they leave for a cruise in the North Atlantic, Enid and Alfred are supposed to have lunch with Chip and Denise. The plan goes awry almost immediately, when Chip returns to his apartment and discovers his girlfriend moving her things out. Chip follows her out the door and leaves his parents with Denise.

We learn that Chip was a tenure-track professor until his college fired him for having a sexual relationship with a female undergrad. Chip has a doctorate in the field of "textual artifacts," and he now subleases an apartment in New York City to pursue a career in screenwriting. Franzen offers a devastating satire of the culture of English departments at colleges and universities. In this privileged academic world, professors try to glamorize themselves with absurd titles like Professor of Textual Artifacts. Why someone who simply teaches Shakespeare needs such an elaborate title is anyone's guess.

One reason Chip chases his girlfriend, Julia, is that he's using her to gain access to her boss, Eden Procuro, a producer of independent films. Chip has written a script, "The Academy Purple," that begins with a long academic monologue on "anxieties of the phallus in Tudor drama" and contains an inordinate number of references to breasts. As a parting shot,

The Corrections

Julia points out the deficiencies in the screenplay, prompting Chip to run off to retrieve the script. Chip's dash through the rain has the slapstick quality of a Charlie Chaplin movie.

Chip encounters his younger sister, Denise, on the street in front of his apartment and tells her she now has to host their parents for lunch. Before he runs off to Eden Procuro, Chip tells Denise, "There's a major, quick set of corrections I have to make." Chip promises to return before Enid and Alfred leave for their cruise ship, but typically he doesn't make it. As Denise prepares lunch for her parents, Enid confesses that she hid a letter from the Axon Corporation, which has been trying to contact Alfred to buy the rights to a chemical process he patented in the 1960s. Enid thinks Axon is trying to take advantage of Alfred by offering him only $5,000 for the patent. But Alfred, who is losing his mental capacities to Parkinson's, just wants to sign the Axon papers and rid himself of any

> *"Now that he had cash in his pocket, a roll of thirty hundreds, he didn't care so much what his parents thought of him."*

responsibilities to the patent. Denise seems to support her father's decision. But Enid explains that her oldest son, Gary, thinks the patent is worth a lot more than Axon's offer and wants to try to negotiate a better deal. Enid likes this idea. She feels perpetually insecure both emotionally and financially, and at the moment, she focuses her anxiety on the Axon offer.

Enid then proposes that Denise and her brothers return to St. Jude for Christmas. The mother and daughter discuss the probability of getting both Gary and Chip to travel home. Denise promises her mother she'll try to persuade her brothers to go. So far in the novel, Denise seems to be the sanest and most levelheaded member of the family. We could see her even enjoying Christmas at home. But the idea of a leather-clad Chip prancing around St. Jude seems ridiculous.

While his parents have lunch at his apartment, Chip makes his way through the rain to Eden Procuro's office. When he arrives, he meets

Julia's husband, Gitanas Misevicius, the recently deposed former deputy prime minister of Lithuania. Gitanas has a plan to use the Internet to scam western investors into sending funds to Lithuania, but he needs someone to write and produce the website for him. Eden gushes that Chip would be ideal for the job, but she says so mainly because she knows it would get Chip out of Julia's life.

Gitanas and Chip strike a deal. The two men leave to pick up Chip's things at his apartment and then fly to Lithuania—a preposterous journey clearly destined for disaster. With these developments, Chip's chances of making it to St. Jude for Christmas seem slim.

THE MORE HE THOUGHT ABOUT IT, THE ANGRIER HE GOT

The focus now shifts to Gary, the oldest son. Gary feels great pressure to conform to others' expectations. Almost everyone contends with this challenge in some capacity in his or her life, but Gary's response is particularly extreme. He seems the ultimate sad sack, the kind of person who spends his life trying to please everyone but ends up pleasing no one—not even himself. The consequences of Gary's struggle are sad but funny.

In our first glimpse of Gary, he's fighting what his wife, Caroline, calls clinical depression, but what Gary calls pressure from his wife and kids to conform to their unrealistic ideals. In short, Caroline and the kids' ideal is complete and utter separation from Gary's parents—the in-laws aren't exactly Caroline's favorites. This animosity leaves Gary torn between pleasing his parents and pleasing his own family. Perhaps this conflict explains why he tries to exert control in his life by taking over the Axon negotiations from his mother. Gary desperately wants to prove to his father that he's worthy of admiration and respect. In some ways, deep in the back of his mind, Gary imagines that this success will be the turning point for his depression—all he needs to do is prove himself to his father, and everything will be fine. His wife and kids will love him, and he'll finally be happy and satisfied. Gary's desperate actions turn the story into farce.

Gary comes across as even more of a loser because he fails all the challenges that face him. First, he tries to negotiate a better deal for his father with the Axon Corporation, but Alfred has already gone ahead and signed over the patent rights for the paltry $5,000 that Axon initially offered. This action further isolates Gary from his father. Nonetheless, Gary barrels onward and attends Axon's pre-IPO presentation. Gary attends mainly to try to get some leverage to renegotiate his father's deal. But Denise joins Gary at the meeting and redirects his efforts when she learns that Axon intends to use Alfred's patent to develop a medical technology, called Corecktall, that allegedly reverses the effects of Parkinson's disease. Gary tries to land his father a spot in the test study for Corecktall, but only wins a promise that the corporation will *consider* Alfred as a candidate. Because this failure takes place in front of his little sister, Gary feels even more humiliated. He feels that, as the older brother, he should be the new patriarch, the one in control—which he's clearly not. The lengths to which he goes to appear in control only heighten the absurdity.

> The lengths Gary goes to in his attempt to appear in control only heighten the absurdity.

Gary next tries to prove himself by getting in on the Axon IPO before other investors do. But the only thing Gary learns in his attempt is how little clout he has with brokerage firms. When he's told he can buy only one-tenth the number of shares he wants, he has only one choice—to crawl to his wife, who has the financial muscle in the family because of her inheritance. But this option is out of the question because of his strained relations with Caroline. She still thinks he's depressed and needs treatment; he still thinks she's just trying to get rid of him. Gary finds himself alone, unable to affirm the least bit of his manhood.

This trend continues as Gary tries to get Caroline and the kids to agree to spend Christmas in St. Jude. For the past eight years, Caroline has insisted that she would never step foot in Enid and Alfred's home again. No amount of campaigning can get her or Gary's two older boys to change their minds. At this point, Gary starts to drink far more than he should and then goes out to trim the hedge with a power tool—a true masculinity-affirming endeavor. But he misses the hedge and cuts a big slice in his hand. Like Chip's journey to his producer's office, Gary's hedge trimming plays out like pure slapstick, a Jerry Lewis routine.

Embarrassed by his stupidity—and stumbling drunk—Gary tries to hide the injury from his wife and kids, a last-ditch effort to maintain some dignity. After so much failure, though, Gary is truly beaten down.

The next morning, hungover and utterly defeated, Gary feels boxed into a corner. He can't turn to his parents, since they aren't capable of helping even themselves. His energy gone, he feels he has to admit to Caroline that she's right. The only other option, running away completely, is pointless. Under these circumstances Gary breaks down and asks his wife for help. He admits he's depressed, hoping for some peace of mind. This correction seems to be a relief, even though it forces Gary to give in completely to his wife's agenda. Is this good or bad? Franzen doesn't judge Gary's choice—he simply presents the puzzle. In any case, the correction makes it possible for Gary to spend Christmas in St. Jude without tearing his family apart. The final irony is that Gary is forced to admit that his attempts to control his life have failed. In short, he has to emasculate himself to find harmony.

AT SEA

This is Alfred's section. Set primarily at sea, this part of the novel follows Enid and Alfred's cruise in the North Atlantic. A cruise is an apt metaphor for Alfred and his state of mind. He's clearly unmoored from the shores of reality, mentally at sea. In contrast to Gary's almost too-real life, Alfred's world is adrift in pure delusion. His consciousness is populated by talking turds and a desperation to return those turds to their point of origin. In this way, "At Sea" has a cartoonish quality that makes for an absurdity that verges on silliness.

The book opens with Alfred and Enid asleep in a stateroom on the ship, but the narrative quickly turns to the past, when the seeds of their marital tension were sown. We finally see the extent of unhappiness in Enid and Alfred's marriage and the frustration each feels in the relationship. The young Enid is a striver. Wanting a better life, she tries to pressure Alfred to invest in the stock of a rival railroad that Midland Pacific is about to buy. Alfred believes doing so would be unethical, and he refuses. Even worse, to spite Enid, he gives the stock tip to a neighbor, who becomes rich from the investment.

The Corrections

The bitterness between Enid and Alfred is plain. At a certain point in their marriage, Alfred discovers a skill that's particularly effective for coping with his unhappiness at home—he sleeps. Franzen calls Alfred's naps "his new lover." Alfred dozes in the evenings after the nightly news. He sleeps on weekend afternoons. Amid the boredom of the symphony or the theater, he finds sleep to be the perfect antidote. Family vacations in the summer are much more bearable if he can nap while Enid drives and hushes the children. Best of all, Enid has no recourse against Alfred's tactic as long as he doesn't doze during dinner parties.

With this new knowledge of Enid's and Alfred's psyches, we return to their stateroom on the cruise ship. It's the middle of the night, and Alfred's Parkinson's is clearly flaring up. He's awake, hallucinating that turds are attacking him. He tries to fight them, then covers the floor with adult diapers and hides in the shower. Enid at first ignores Alfred's mania because she wants to maintain the fiction that everything is all right. Finally, she can't. She spends nights without sleep, battling Alfred and his delusions, while during the day she tries to maintain a sense of normalcy. Ironically, the one friend Enid makes on the cruise is using the trip to escape the memory of her daughter's murder. Enid listens to this sad story and offers her sympathy, but is unable to open up reciprocally and share her frustration with Alfred's illness.

Sinking the love boat

Enid and Alfred's cruise in **The Corrections** recalls a memorable piece by one of Franzen's contemporaries, the novelist and essayist David Foster Wallace. In 1995, **Harper's** magazine sent Wallace on an all-expense-paid Caribbean cruise, hoping he could provide some highbrow insight into the American cultural phenomenon that is the luxury cruise vacation. The result was the hilariously cynical page-turner "A Supposedly Fun Thing I'll Never Do Again." Wallace hated the cruise. In the course of the ninety-page essay, Wallace navigates the "Syrianly tan" throngs of tourists crowding an airport terminal that "resembles the fall of Saigon," faces the dangers of the ship's vacuum toilets—so powerful that "your waste seems less removed than *hurled* from you"—and picks apart the "fiendish" cruise-vacation brochures that leave you feeling "you will *have no choice* but to have a good time."

Enid's dilemma would be tragic if smart-alecky turds weren't attacking Alfred. Luckily for Enid, Alfred is fairly lucid during the daylight hours and goes to bed early. Enid also finds help from the ship's doctor, who gives her a drug that has qualities similar to Ecstasy. With a few doses of the drug down the hatch, Enid glides through the rest of the trip. For the first time in her life, she doesn't feel self-conscious. Enid's correction is this little pill that magically seems to resolve all of life's difficulties.

Alfred finds his own correction at the end of this section by taking a headlong plunge off the upper deck of the ship into the ocean. He disappears into the "wine-dark sea"—an allusion to Homer's *Odyssey* that conveys the confused and muddled nature of Alfred's thoughts and suggests ominous things to come.

THE GENERATOR

Franzen starts "The Generator" with what appears to be a digression but that quickly leads into Denise's story. Why Franzen begins with this detour, aside from its amusing qualities, is unclear. Consequently, this section doesn't begin like the others. Instead of meeting Denise outright, we back into her life. If Chip hadn't impulsively left for Lithuania (which we read about later), Denise would have the most dramatic personal life of anyone in the family. Not only is she a star chef, she's sexually adventurous to boot. In a sense, Denise lives for pleasure, and she's narrowed it down to two kinds—food and sex. For some this might be healthy and refreshingly simple, but for Denise it's disastrous.

The digression at the beginning of this section focuses on Robin Passafaro, the daughter of a "family of troublemakers and true believers." She has uncles in the mob and in the Teamsters. Her father is a socialist schoolteacher. Her adopted brother, Billy, is a psychotic criminal, currently in prison for attacking an executive with a baseball bat and leaving him severely disabled. But Robin and her husband, Brian, are astoundingly rich. Brian invented a new technology and sold it to the W— Corporation, a huge software conglomerate, for close to $20 million. The catch is that the man Robin's brother attacked and maimed was the vice president of that same W—Corporation, the very source of Robin and Brian's financial bliss.

The Corrections

This bizarre situation has very different effects on Robin and Brian. Robin retreats to Catholicism for comfort and consolation, plagued by guilt for what her brother has done. Brian, on the other hand, feels no guilt. In fact, his sale to the W—Corporation only reinforces his sense of privilege in the world. He had gone to the best schools, married the prettiest coed, and sold his startup company for a fortune. Now he can afford to indulge his every whim. His only limitation is that he has to indulge these whims exclusively in Philadelphia because Robin refuses to move. So Brian decides to bring to Philadelphia the things he desires. The first item he wants is a first-class restaurant. This is where Denise, the youngest Lambert, comes in. She's Philadelphia's hottest chef, so Brian offers her the chance to develop her own restaurant with his financial backing. He pays for her to travel Europe to research the finest restaurants and cuisine.

At this point, Franzen takes us on a tour of Denise's past, focusing on her sex life. He reveals that although Denise's life seems perfect on the surface, her personal life is a bit stormy. She has been involved with three different men who were at least twice her age. The first two were married; the third she married. But that marriage ended when Denise became involved with a woman.

After the digression, Franzen returns to the present and to Denise and Brian's growing relationship. Denise's opportunity is every ambitious chef's dream come true. Brian shows Denise an abandoned generator building on the waterfront just south of Center City Philadelphia. He offers to renovate the building and turn it into a restaurant while Denise is traveling in Europe. Brian also offers to join her there for two weeks, an idea Denise likes very much. But before she leaves, she wants to meet Brian's family, so he invites her out to his weekend house in Cape May, New Jersey. There, Denise meets Robin and the kids. Robin seems indifferent, almost hostile, toward Denise. This animosity culminates when Denise cooks a fabulous meal, only to learn that Robin had already prepared dinner.

Not long afterward, Brian tries to seduce Denise during the trip to Europe. She initially feels willing but quickly has second thoughts, afraid of getting involved with yet another married man. When they return to Philadelphia, Denise quietly pursues a friendship with Robin—whether out of guilt or desire, she doesn't really know. As Denise breaks through Robin's hostility and establishes a friendship, she becomes a part of

Robin and Brian's family. Denise baby-sits for the girls and often eats dinner at their house. Brian, on the other hand, begins to pursue other interests, particularly in the movie industry. Though he still keeps his promises about the restaurant, he becomes less and less visible in Denise's life, while Robin's presence increases. Inevitably, Denise ends up wanting to sleep with Robin but is so embarrassed by her feelings that she immerses herself in the business of opening the restaurant in order to escape. Eventually, the restaurant, called the Generator, opens to rave reviews. Denise becomes a culinary star in the region, with publications left and right naming the Generator as the best new restaurant on the eastern seaboard.

> *"She'd never seen so objectively what an illness sex was, what a collection of bodily symptoms, because she'd never been remotely as sick as Robin made her."*

On the heels of this success, Denise seduces Robin, who is a willing participant. They have a torrid affair that subsides only when Brian almost catches them. As the stress of the affair becomes too much for either woman to endure, they grow distant from each other. Denise again loses herself in her work at the restaurant, while Robin returns to religion. Surprisingly, Robin's new devotion leads Brian to divorce her. To make things more complicated, Brian spends the night with Denise after telling her of his intention to divorce. Early the next morning, Robin arrives on Denise's doorstep but for some reason fails to notice Brian's car on the street in front. Denise manages to shuffle Robin out the door, at which point the phone rings—it's Gary, informing her that their father has fallen off the cruise ship into the sea. But in the blink of an eye, Robin returns, having spotted the car. She storms past Denise into the bedroom. After several minutes of yelling, Robin leaves. As Brian leaves moments later, he tells Denise that she's fired.

Now, not only is Denise's personal life a mess, but this mess has spilled into her professional life, causing her to get fired from the best job she ever had. Franzen seems to take perverse pleasure in Denise's downfall, which makes for very funny reading. The correction in Denise's life takes the form of personal and professional humiliation. This correction is the change that makes it possible for Denise to return to St. Jude for Christmas.

With Denise's correction complete, only Chip's remains. Franzen turns his focus to Lithuania, where Chip is living in a rent-free villa and enjoying the nightlife of Vilnius. Things are going so well in his campaign to scam Internet investors that Chip doesn't plan to return to the U.S. until the spring. He writes an e-mail to Denise apologizing that he won't be able to make Christmas in St. Jude. Denise responds by demanding that he attend. He ignores her entreaties and settles into the Wild West lifestyle of the newly opened free markets of eastern Europe. The good fortune doesn't last, however. A coup overthrows the provisional Lithuanian government, and Chip and Misevicius have to get out

> The **correction** in Denise's life **takes** the form of **personal** and professional **humiliation.**

of town fast. Chip heads for the airport and tries to catch a flight when the entire infrastructure of the city collapses. Ironically, the coup operates as a form of correction for Chip that forces him to return home, perhaps in time for Christmas.

By the end of "The Generator," the plot hums deliciously over the incredible difficulties in which the Lamberts find themselves in. Like most Christmas fables, the elaborate conflicts and complications all lead to the Lambert's doorstep with crisp, ironic holiday cheer.

ONE LAST CHRISTMAS

As a result of the Lamberts' minor individual corrections, the family is now on a collision course for Christmas in St. Jude. "One Last Christmas" begins with Alfred once again in his basement sanctuary, untangling strings of Christmas lights and fussing with replacement bulbs. Along with the strings of lights, Alfred also has retrieved his shotgun and locked it in his workshop. He knows that his Parkinson's is worsening and laments the fact that he didn't have the courage to let himself drown in the ocean after falling off the cruise ship. He now hopes he can summon the courage to shoot himself and finally finish things. In this lucid moment, Alfred realizes his destiny is a nursing home. This is not the way he imagined his life ending.

The story then turns to Enid. Her newly discovered coping tool is Aslan, the Ecstasy-like drug the ship's doctor "prescribed" for her. (Aslan is also the name of the heroic lion from C.S. Lewis's *The Chronicles of Narnia*, which one of Gary's sons reads throughout *The Corrections*.) The pills eased Enid through the terrible humiliation of Alfred's cruise-ship accident and carried her back to St. Jude on a euphoric cloud. Enid's withdrawal from the drug, however, is severe. She almost dies from the delayed shame. The pills aren't available in the U.S., so Enid devises a scheme to get them. Her neighbor is going to Austria to visit her daughter and son-in-law, who is a doctor. Enid asks her friend to bring back a six-month supply.

While Enid awaits her drug score, she worries about Alfred being accepted into the Corecktall test program. If Alfred shows any signs of dementia, he's automatically ineligible for the Corecktall trial. The signs of dementia are all there, but Enid only wants to deny, deny, deny. A hit of Aslan would certainly ease the stress of this denial.

Two days before Christmas, Gary arrives at his parents' house, unaccompanied. Enid is disappointed that Gary's youngest son didn't come along as planned. Gary is determined to play the role of the oldest son and newly minted patriarch during his time in St. Jude, but his earlier correction makes it difficult for him to stay the course. His first resolution is to convince his parents to sell their house and move into an apartment, but he's never quite able to make his argument. In the meantime, Gary answers the door when Enid's neighbor delivers the Aslan pills. Afraid his mother might become addicted, Gary hides them.

Denise arrives the next day, unsure whether to take a new job in New York City or stay in Philadelphia. Gary tells Denise about Enid's pills. Following the recent pattern, Gary sees his authority undermined when Denise steals the pills and gives them to Enid. But Enid, pills in hand, decides to wash them down the drain rather than start taking them again. In a sense, this action reverses her earlier correction. But Gary doesn't seem to learn anything from his mother's turnaround. He still tries to maintain an iron fist over his parents and ends the Christmas holiday with some nasty words on the morning of his departure.

While this touching holiday scene is taking place in St. Jude, Chip is on a wild ride from the Vilnius airport to the Polish border. Captured by masked Lithuanian "police," he is stripped and most of his money is stolen. He is left with just enough money to make it back to St. Jude. The Christmas that Enid was so intent on orchestrating finally happens, but it's clearly a letdown after everything that's taken place.

"One Last Christmas" ends as Alfred enters the hospital to be evaluated for dementia. It's clear right away that Alfred will never leave assisted care. Surprisingly, Alfred reaches out to Chip, who promises to extend his

> *"The question was: How to get out of this prison?"*

stay in St. Jude to help his father make the transition to the hospital. This act of generosity changes Chip's life. Helpless in his hospital bed, Alfred remembers the question he's been wanting to ask Chip. He asks Chip to kill him and help him end things, but Chip refuses. This is one correction that neither Chip nor anyone else can make.

THE CORRECTIONS

The final section is an epilogue that tells how each of the characters' lives turn out after their respective corrections. Enid finally finds real happiness alone in her home, free from the burden of taking care of Alfred all day, every day. The anxieties that had plagued her life seem trivial now that Alfred is out the picture. Chip stays in the area and becomes involved with Alfred's neurologist. They marry and have twins. Chip stays home with the kids and writes, while his new wife joins a practice in the Chicago suburbs. This suburban idyll is about as far away from Chip's self-involved, hipster lifestyle as possible.

Gary returns home to his family. He takes a bath on the Axon Corporation's poor IPO and settles back into his conventional life. His correction is a shift of focus from his old family—his parents—toward the one he lives with every day—his wife and kids. Denise moves to Brooklyn and becomes head chef at a hot new restaurant. With her correction, she simplifies her life and avoids confronting her sexuality.

Finally, about two years after entering the nursing home, Alfred begins to refuse food and makes the ultimate correction. He lasts longer than anyone expects, and all his children are able to visit him before he dies. In the end, life goes on—but less turbulently.

The Corrections We Make

Franzen shows us how each of our lives is a series of corrections—our attempts to correct the faults of our parents and the mistakes of our pasts.

○ ○ ○

ALFRED MAKES THE ULTIMATE CORRECTION

If we measure corrections by the degree to which they change a person's life, Alfred's is the biggest one—the ultimate correction. By the end of the book he's dead. Conscious of the progression of his Parkinson's, Alfred spends much of the novel passively observing his own creeping death. In a sense, he gave up life years before, when he descended into a deep depression and coped with it by sleeping as much as possible. In his retirement years, he spent most of his time in the basement, which suggests that he already resided in a grave of sorts. It was only a matter of time before it was formalized.

Still, the choice of whether to die or not is difficult for Alfred. When the opportunity to die arrives serendipitously when he tumbles off the deck of the cruise ship, Alfred can't allow himself just to relax and let nature take its course. He instinctively swims and allows himself to be rescued. To everyone's surprise, Alfred's spill into the North Atlantic hardly affects him, and he returns home pretty much unchanged.

But not long after, Alfred discovers his old shotgun stored in the basement near the Christmas lights. He had bought the shotgun with the thought of hunting when he retired, but his first attempt at using it convinced him that hunting wasn't a good pastime for him. While repairing the Christmas lights, he pulls out the shotgun and a box of shells. He contemplates using the gun but places the weapon in his workshop, perhaps to pull the trigger later. Still, Alfred is unable to blow himself away. He simply doesn't have the courage to take his own life. When Gary and

> *"The odd truth about Alfred was that love, for him, was a matter not of approaching but of keeping away."*

Denise discover the gun, Alfred's plan is exposed, making the possibility of taking his own life impossible.

Days later, when Alfred is hospitalized to determine if he's eligible for the Corecktall trial, the opportunity to take his own life has effectively passed. Not only is he strapped to his hospital bed, he now also lacks the lucidity to act on his own. But Alfred still has the mental wherewithal to plead with Chip—seemingly his most heartless and self-involved son—to kill him. Chip, of course, is unable to do so. While Chip's response leads to his own correction, Alfred must endure. It's only when Alfred has completely lost his faculties that something in him finds the courage to go on a hunger strike, which to everyone's surprise lasts much longer than expected. It's as if death is difficult even when Alfred chooses to die.

CHIP TURNS HIS LIFE AROUND COMPLETELY

At the beginning of the novel, Chip's life is on a trajectory far different from the one on which he ends up. He lives the life of an arty intellectual, an avid reader of Foucault and Marx. He decries "commercialized, medicalized, totalitarian modernity" while pursuing women and going into crippling debt. His screenplay seems to have two dominant themes—breasts and the "anxieties of the phallus in Tudor drama." Chip sounds incredibly full of himself. But maybe that's what earning a degree in "textual artifacts" does to you. Though it is clear that Chip is just an English professor, the implication is that he's hipper than ordinary English teachers, a Superman to all those Clark Kents. Chip doesn't just save the world from knotty literature, he unravels the secrets of every kind of text—from Shakespeare's *Troilus and Cressida* to your mom's to-do list.

Chip seems to have no motivations beyond the pursuit of personal gratification. In completely self-centered fashion, he unthinkingly lurches from one pleasurable experience to another. He's the kind of person you want to grab by the shoulders and shout, "Think it through! What are the consequences?" This pursuit of pleasure gets Chip involved in the Internet scam in Lithuania. He finds himself dumped by his girl-friend, horribly in debt, and promoting an incredibly stupid screenplay. He deals with his problems by heading for the hills, leaving the country and himself in the economic free-for-all of Lithuania, which means sex, drugs, and cash—lots of cash. As a character in this novel, Chip is proba-bly the one most in need of an attitude adjustment, a major correction.

When Chip is stripped of everything he has earned (if you can call ripping off investors "earning"), we're relieved. It's in this state that Chip arrives in St. Jude for Christmas. By losing everything—his dignity, his money, his reputation—Chip becomes ready for his correction. His cor-rection teaches him to empathize. It's much like Dr. Seuss's famous Christmas story in which the Grinch's "small heart / Grew three sizes" on Christmas day. Chip's heart grows when he agrees to stay and help his father in the hospital. This first act of selflessness inspires Chip so much so that he even starts dating his father's doctor.

Chip's correction is so extraordinary that he changes into another per-son. Chip represents the extreme in psychological correction.

ENID FINDS TRUE HAPPINESS

For most of the novel, Enid is the embodiment of the bitter, powerless housewife. She spends every day trying to survive under Alfred's negative, harshly judging gaze. She lives in fear of his criticism and therefore goes to extreme measures to keep order in the house. She takes her role of household manager so seriously that she keeps a tight rein on expenses and makes sure the magazines on the coffee table are fanned evenly. Enid takes pride in her coupon clipping and stays prepared for any potential savings on a purchase. But she has reached a stage in her life when her coupon clipping has become compulsive. She saves every coupon, even the useless, expired ones.

Because Enid feels so powerless in her own home, she never confronts her anger directly. Enid's only choice is to be passive-aggressive. When the children still lived at home, Enid would serve liver for dinner on the pretense that it was "healthy"—fully aware that Alfred hated liver with a passion. Later, she redecorated the den, banishing Alfred's prized leather chair to the basement because it didn't fit with the new décor.

The one instance when Enid did attempt to initiate something ended in disaster. She tried to prod Alfred to invest in the stock of the Erie Belt Railroad. The request was somewhat unethical, though, because Enid and Alfred had inside information that Alfred's company was about to acquire Erie Belt. Enid simply asked Alfred to use this knowledge to pad the family's finances. When Alfred refused, she even tried to coerce him with sexual favors. Enid's actions made Alfred so angry that he leaked the information to a neighbor out of pure spite. The neighbor made a killing on the investment while Enid and Alfred made nothing.

This episode shows us that Alfred interpreted any overt action on Enid's part as a form of emasculation. His response was always quick and decisive. Alfred never had sex with Enid again—not that the sex was ever that great

The hero of the book

"I think Enid's the hero of the book. At the outset it's infuriating how hopeful she is in the face of obvious grave troubles. It comes off as an annoying inability to face reality, and yet, ultimately her hope is one of the most beautiful things about her. . . . [H]ope is one of the primary Christian virtues— faith, hope, and charity. Enid struggles very hard with charity, and she has some little crises of faith, but she never loses hope. If you have a literature that is built around the tragic recognition that there's always going to be pain and suffering—no way to escape that—it sure helps if you can introduce some note of hope as well. I think that's true to my experience of life."

Jonathan Franzen, interview with the *Atlantic,* October 2001 anyway. Alfred's idea of sex was to edge up to Enid while she was asleep and quickly copulate from behind. No foreplay, no mutual gratification.

As a result of her stifled married life, Enid is incredibly insecure about her finances and her social standing. We see this insecurity in her behavior on the cruise ship, where in a sense she can be whoever she wants to be. She is unmoored from her real life and can invent a persona—one that can be friends with doctors' wives, rich Europeans, and other people who seem exotic to her.

As the novel progresses, it becomes painfully clear that Enid is in dire need of a correction. But her correction isn't death or a complete change of circumstances. Enid simply needs to overcome her insecurity. She accomplishes this feat in two stages. First, Enid discovers that she can be free when she takes Aslan, an Ecstasy-like drug that's illegal in the U.S. but perfectly legal on the high seas. The cruise ship's doctor gives her Aslan, and the results are miraculous. With the drug, nothing bothers Enid—not even the humiliation of her husband's dive off the ship into the North Atlantic. The drug works so well that, back in St. Jude, Enid schemes to score a six-month supply from a friend vactationing in Europe. But by the time her friend returns, Enid has come to terms with her own insecurities and no longer needs "mother's little helper."

The second stage of Enid's correction is her newfound enjoyment of life once Alfred is gone from her daily existence. Her financial and social troubles are gone. Without Alfred constantly putting her in fear of emotional or verbal attack, Enid finally is able to see that her life is really not that bad. She has plenty of money and the friends she wants. She can even cultivate her more appealing traits, like her loving and generous nature. The result is a more tolerant, carefree Enid. She enjoys being "carried around the room while the klezmer music played" at Chip's wedding. When she decides to end a forty-year friendship with a homophobic neighbor, Enid lends unspoken and perhaps unknowing support to her lesbian daughter. This kind of acceptance enables Enid to enjoy true happiness for the first time in her life.

DENISE DISCOVERS A FATHER'S LOVE

On the surface, Denise's correction appears to be simply a change of scene, from Philadelphia to Brooklyn. At the end of the novel, she's still a star chef, the same job she's had all along. Her sexuality is still unresolved. She believes she is a lesbian, but isn't completely able to accept it. What changes in Denise is her understanding of her relationship with her father. When we first meet her, she is friendly toward Alfred, preparing him his own plate of appetizers in Chip's apartment in New York. Alfred, however, appears remote, barely noticing his daughter. At first, we think this is the result of Parkinson's—but once we learn about Denise's earlier actions as a young woman, we think otherwise.

> **Denise's** correction helps **her realize** the **depth** of **love** her **seemingly** **cold father** **truly** feels **for her.**

In the summer after her high school graduation, she works a summer job in the Signals Department of her father's railroad company. The department is composed of a dozen middle-aged men. Don Armour, a depressed Vietnam vet, is the only one in the department who doesn't seem to like Denise. But after a period of aloofness, Don Armour approaches her. Denise feels a sense of pity that attracts her to him. In no time she sleeps with him in her own room at home when her parents are away. After sex, Armour leaves Denise in her girlhood bed. A year later, the summer after her freshman year in college, Denise carries on a secret and torrid affair with with the father of one of her college roommates. The affair is exciting but crazy, for the man is terrified of being caught. He takes Denise to out-of-the-way ethnic restaurants in Queens where she learns to love food and finds her calling. In both affairs, Denise appears to be seeking the affections of older men not simply to compensate for the lack of attention from her father, but also because these men seemed to need her like her father did not.

During her Christmas visit to St. Jude, Denise finally learns the real reason her father abruptly quit his job from Midland Pacific, condemning himself to a substantially reduced pension. Denise discovers that when a rival company purchased Midland Pacific, Alfred was offered a job at substantially higher pay to help with the transition before he retired. To everyone's surprise, especially Enid's, he declined the job without explanation.

At Christmas, Alfred explains to Denise that he quit because Don Armour was blackmailing him. At the time of the sale, Don Armour approached Alfred and threatened to expose the affair with Denise, which would humiliate Alfred and ruin Denise's reputation. Don Armour promised to keep quiet if Alfred guaranteed him a job in the new company. Alfred's rigid sense of ethics made the situation impossible: he couldn't give in to the request, but also couldn't tolerate any public revelations. So Alfred quit, leaving Don Armour without any leverage. Alfred kept this a secret for years to spare Denise, but now, at Christmas, the moment seems appropriate to tell her.

With this news, Denise finally understands how much her father has been willing to sacrifice his own well-being for her comfort. This correction helps Denise realize the depth of love her seemingly cold father truly feels for her. This knowledge makes her an even stronger advocate for her parents and their wishes. She convinces Chip to stay in St. Jude after she returns to Philadelphia. On the surface, this correction doesn't change Denise's life in a significant way, but it gives her the peace and security she's been searching for over the years in the arms of older men.

GARY MAKES THE BIGGEST SACRIFICE—HIS SOUL

When we meet Gary, he has achieved everything he was raised to do. He has a powerful job as a bank vice president. He's married to a rich and beautiful wife. He has three smart sons who appear to be on their way to success of their own. He has a large home in the most exclusive section of Philadelphia. But the façade of perfection crumbles when we get a glimpse of life inside the home. Gary lives inside a nightmare marriage. His wife, Caroline, is more Mephistopheles than June Cleaver. In Christopher Marlowe's *Dr. Faustus* (and Goethe's *Faustus*), Mephistopheles is a devil who lures unsuspecting people into trading their souls for what they

The Corrections

desire the most. In these works, a man named Faust sells his soul to Mephistopheles in exchange for youth, knowledge, and magical power. For the promise of immediate gratification Faust is willing to accept eternal damnation. *The Corrections* gives us a more contemporary twist on this tale, as Gary finds himself faced with the prospect of trading his soul—or, more accurately, his sense of self—for the prize of family harmony.

Gary is torn between what he knows to be true and what his wife wants him to believe. We first meet Gary in the photography studio Caroline has built for him over the garage. The studio is not something Gary particularly wanted, but Caroline claims it's what he's been dreaming of always. To avoid confrontation, Gary embarks on a project of reprinting old photographs to create a Lambert family photo album. Watching his family playing soccer in the backyard, he notices Caroline reinjure her back. Shortly after, the phone rings, and Caroline runs to answer it and trips on the steps. It's Enid calling to invite Gary and family to Christmas in St. Jude—a place Caroline has vowed never to set foot in again. Gary and Caroline's ensuing conflict about the Christmas trip devolves into a he-said-she-said argument over Caroline's injury. She claims she reinjured her back while running to answer Enid's call. He argues that she hurt herself playing soccer with the kids. The disagreement becomes emblematic of the constant power struggle the two wage.

Caroline marshals all her ammunition against Gary. She enlists their boys in mocking Gary and his parents. She uses the argument to further press her position that Gary is depressed—simply because he won't do

A set of corrections

"[Gary's] done all the things expected of him while also attempting not to repeat the mistakes his parents made. . . . His father was a ferocious worker, Gary's very strict about only 40 hours per week. While his father was very strict with his children, Gary is permissive, and where his father dominated his mother, Gary is more or less dominated by his wife. So right down the line, a set of corrections. I wouldn't want to sign off on the idea that it's just as unhappy a marriage, but it speaks to the idea that there's no gain without loss and almost no loss without potential gain. That's a spirit that animates the whole book."

Jonathan Franzen, interview in *Salon,* September 7, 2001

what she wants. In response, Gary begins to drink heavily, which makes his depression even worse. Compounding the tension, Gary is convinced that he can make a killing on the IPO of the Axon Corporation, the biotech firm that bought his father's patent. To Gary's extreme regret, he doesn't have enough influence to persuade investment firms to sell him the number of shares he wants. These firms sell special offers only to their biggest clients—and Gary isn't one. The only way for Gary to make the purchase is to ask for Caroline's help, since she's rich and has a substantial investment portfolio. But to get on Caroline's good side, Gary has to admit that he's wrong and she's right.

The conflict comes to a head on a night when Gary has a few too many drinks and then goes outside in a desperate attempt to salvage his masculinity by trimming the hedge with some power tools. He cuts himself badly and retreats to his bedroom. The next morning, he's too depressed to get up. Caroline has withdrawn all her emotional support and turned the kids against him. Gary's only options are to move out and be alone or succumb to Caroline's agenda and be part of the family again. The choice seems obvious to Gary. He admits that she's right. Yes, he's depressed. He'll do anything she wants, even sacrifice what he believes for the sake of family harmony.

In the short run, Gary finds himself back in the warm embrace of his wife and children, but the price he pays is that he must shut down a big part of himself. We don't see the long-term consequences of Gary's sacrifice of his integrity for this immediate gratification. We probably wouldn't be surprised, though, to see Gary become as repressed as his father was.

Bringing It All Back Home

Looking past the media storm, what do readers of *The Corrections* really think about the novel?

○ ○ ○

Is all the hype worth it? Is *The Corrections* really that important a novel?

"YES—IT'S THE GREAT AMERICAN NOVEL FOR THE NEW MILLENNIUM."

In Franzen's now famous essay "Perchance to Dream," which appeared in *Harper's* magazine in 1996, he wrote that he wanted to "Address the Culture and Bring News to the Mainstream" (the capital letters are his). In *The Corrections*, he brings to life large social issues of our day through a sprawling story of an American family past its prime. But the Lamberts don't face the traditional conflicts of realist novels—war, famine, social unrest, poverty, and so on. Their plight is one of abundance. In a country where obesity has reached epidemic proportions, Franzen's concerns ring true.

On the surface, the Lamberts have achieved the American dream. The father held a mid-level executive position with a railroad company and is now retired with a pension. The mother was a stay-at-home mom and embodied the image of homemaker that the American media celebrated at the time. Their children grew up in the suburbs, attending good public schools and excelling. Now the individual family members' lives have outgrown the myths of *Leave It to Beaver, Ozzie and Harriet,* and *Father Knows Best.* They're left with no models to define themselves. They're all adrift, just as our culture is adrift now that these earlier ideals have proven unworkable.

The Corrections turns on a well-worn, almost sitcom-like plot conflict: will Mom get the family home for one last Christmas? While this situation does produce a thin veneer of comedy, beneath its surface lies an agonizing anxiety about the American dream of happy family life. Each of the characters has to deal with the devastating fact that happiness isn't found where they've been taught to look. In this manner, *The Corrections* confronts the banality and the vacuousness of the American dream. Enid doesn't find happiness in her role as homemaker. Alfred has given up searching for it altogether. Gary doesn't experience it in what appears to be an ideal family. Denise can't achieve it through career success. Only Chip, seemingly the most radical Lambert, finds it once he returns home and engages in an act of charity by taking care of his father in the hospital. There, Chip meets his father's neurologist. They get married, have children, and settle into life in the suburbs. With this outcome, Franzen seems to offer possible redemption—unless Chip is just destined to repeat his parents' disappointments. Franzen doesn't say. We're left with ambiguity, which adds a note of anxiety at the end.

This story is the story that America faces at the end of the nineties and the beginning of the millennium. It raises questions that we must all confront in America's post-prosperity reality. Franzen ingeniously highlights this aspect by drawing comparisons between our personal lives and the stock market by using term for a short-lived drop in stock prices—a correction. We all have to make corrections in our lives to deal with the fact that material things—a suburban home, two cars, a chicken in the oven—don't necessarily last. And even if they do, we can't depend on them for our happiness.

"IT'S A HILARIOUS READ—WHAT MORE CAN YOU POSSIBLY WANT?"

Forget the Great American Novel question—it doesn't matter. *The Corrections* is a truly hilarious book. Why try to make it something more? It's a great read and has some very funny characters and situations. Think

John Kennedy Toole's A *Confederacy of Dunces* rather than William Faulkner's *The Sound and the Fury*. Toole won a Pulitzer Prize for his bizarre, gothic romp through New Orleans, but no one will mistake his very funny book for a great American novel. Franzen performs similar magic, and many elements of *The Corrections* aren't meant to be taken seriously. Chip's roll in the hay with an undergrad and his get-rich-quick trip to eastern Europe are the stuff of comedy, not tragedy.

Franzen ratchets up the plot to a point of such silliness that the novel becomes a farce. Will Enid get her Christmas? Will Alfred kill himself or end up in a nursing home? Will Denise figure out her sexuality? Will Gary finally stand up to his bossy wife and children? The novel reads like a good old potboiler without much to boil. In this sense, Franzen elevates the trivial for comic effect. This comedy makes *The Corrections* a great read, but not much more.

Gitanas Misevicius, the Lithuanian mobster (Is Franzen serious?) says that the situation in his country is one of "tragedy rewritten as farce." When we read this, we nod knowingly. The absurd situations the novel's characters find themselves mired in can only be seen as satire. Chip works for Gitanas creating an Internet scam. Denise is caught between her two lovers—a husband and wife! Alfred pees in Yuban coffee cans and is chased by turds. Gary caves to his wife's interpretation of him even though it's obvious she's a whiny manipulator. Enid's obsession with Hallmark-card perfection as a homemaker is taken to ridiculous heights. In all, the novel is like throwing a firecracker into a barrel of monkeys. If the explosion doesn't make you laugh, the monkeys will.

"IT'S IMPORTANT NOW, BUT IN TEN YEARS, NO."

The Corrections may be causing a stir now, but in ten years nobody will be reading it. It'll go the way of Tom Wolfe's *The Bonfire of the Vanities*, which was a blockbuster in 1987 but has faded since. *The Bonfire of the Vanities* was about the values of greed that dominated 1980s America, and it was published to great acclaim and controversy. Wolfe even wrote his own manifesto reclaiming American fiction in the name of the large social sagas of the nineteenth century. The parallel between Wolfe's book and Franzen's is remarkable. Both novels detail the darker side of the American success story. Both chronicle the utter emptiness of America's success-obsessed culture and especially focus on its East Coast manifestation.

The Corrections

The Bonfire of the Vanities exposes the self-absorbed world of Wall Street "haves" in contrast to the "have-nots" who live just a few miles north in the same city. *The Corrections* contrasts the East Coast cultural "haves" and the Midwest "have-nots." Franzen's book builds on our cultural bias that big eastern cities like Philadelphia and New York are where real living happens, while bland suburban enclaves like St. Jude are culturally and spiritually blank. *The Corrections* exposes the weaknesses behind these assumptions and reinvigorates the myth of the Midwestern small-town idyll. We discover this through the three Lambert children's struggles to find peace. Denise and Gary, who both stay in the East, make compromises that fail to lift them out of their malaise. But Chip performs a complete turnaround, returning home to the Midwest and beginning a conventional suburban life.

Like the characters in *The Bonfire of the Vanities*, those in *The Corrections* has an immediacy to them. Their struggles to find happiness ring true with a generation of people who haven't found satisfaction and are beginning to question the choices they've made in life. But the problem with *The Corrections* is that it's too wrapped up in contemporary conflicts. Ten years from now, nobody will care about these problems because they're not timeless.

From the perspective of fifteen years, we *know* that greed isn't good. We don't need Tom Wolfe to tell us this anymore. In fact, *The Bonfire of the Vanities* seems almost quaint in its moralizing against the big-time financial world. The same will happen to *The Corrections*. A decade from now, the shallowness of East Coast intellectualism will seem like an old story as we tuck our kids in at night after reading *Harry Potter*.

"IT'S A LANDMARK NOVEL, BUT NOT FOR WHAT FRANZEN HOPES."

Critics might praise *The Corrections* as that mythical beast the Great American Novel, but the whole idea of such a novel is like the prize on one of those snipe hunts your cousins sent you on when you were a kid. It doesn't amount to much. It's kind of a last gasp by the Great White Writer. Franzen portrays an aspect of American culture that's already been relegated to the dustbin of history—the white, all-American, Midwestern nuclear family. Today is an age of blended families, and the Lamberts are an anachronism. As a result, they're an easy mark for satire, and not a particularly pertinent one. There's a real "been there, done that" feel to the novel in the way it satirizes the Lamberts' successes and failures. Everybody knows that the suburbs aren't perfect. The pursuit of success is shallow. Material things can't give you happiness. But Franzen trots out all of these tried-and-true themes for one last trip around the track.

On the surface, Franzen seems to be criticizing this world, but by the novel's end, he celebrates the same core values that he started out deriding. Franzen really wants a tidy world where families can be part of a community of people just like them. The only two characters who seem to find peace are Enid, who can finally enjoy home without the complication of her dying husband, and Chip, who's settled into a life much like that of his parents. This is not the world we live in. It's a tidy fantasy, not far from the trite garbage the advertising industry has served up for all these years. At least ad execs have figured out that the world has changed. It's Tiger Woods's world now, not the *Brady Bunch*. Blended families are in. Multiculturalism is the coin of the realm. Franzen's novel is so white and remote from reality that his realism can only be called fantasy.

○ ○ ○

Which characters emerge as winners and losers in *The Corrections*?

"THE MEN FLOP AND THE WOMEN PREVAIL."

The female characters in *The Corrections* emerge triumphant, even the most minor of these characters. The men, on the other hand, lose everything. By the end of the novel, the two main women in the novel, Enid and Denise, achieve seemingly everything they have dreamed. Enid finally finds peace when Alfred moves to a nursing home. All her insecurities about money and social status seem to fade away, as she realizes she has enough money to maintain her home and live comfortably. With this burden lifted, Enid can nourish her innate generosity while at the same time enjoy needling Alfred in the nursing home without fear of consequences.

The Corrections

Denise also is successful, for she finds the acclaim she has dreamed of without the emotional complications that dogged her in the past. In losing her job at the Generator and then moving to a new restaurant in New York City, Denise sheds the complications of sleeping with her boss's wife and finally wins the appreciation of restaurant reviewers and customers she believes she deserves. Throughout the story, Denise has been irked that no one has praised her sauerkraut, but then a *New York Times* profile of her new restaurant finally hits the mark. A job as a chef in New York, the center of the American culinary world, is a huge step up. All the better that this new job isn't complicated by the soap opera gyrations of her Philadelphia restaurant. Life couldn't be better for Denise.

The novel's secondary female characters also prevail. Caroline, Gary's wife, is clearly the most obvious minor character to achieve her goals. She manipulates Gary to give in to her wishes in almost every regard. When Caroline orchestrates a story that Gary is depressed and then sells this story to their children, Gary has to get with her program or hit the road. Gary doesn't want to be alone, so he succumbs to her demands. In addition to Caroline, both Chip's ex-girlfriend Julia Vrais and Julia's boss, Eden Procuro, are successful. Julia not only dumps Chip, but also divorces her Lithuanian husband and gets the apartment he bought with stolen government funds. Eden continues to manage Julia's love life and remain a top-dog producer. Robin Callahan, the only other minor female character of significance, doesn't gain much except freedom from her vacuous, self-involved husband. Even that's not a bad deal—especially considering there may be nice divorce settlement in her future.

Aside from Chip, the men in this novel all lose. Alfred loses his mind, then his life. Gary loses his dignity and sacrifices his sense of justice in order to maintain a family life. Minor characters like Gitanas Misevicius lose everything. On the flight to the Lithuanian–Polish border, Gitanas is stripped of everything he owns. Denise's ex-husband, Emile Berger, takes Denise's place at the Generator, which is like trying to follow Liza Minnelli in *Cabaret* on Broadway. Emile is clearly second best. We might argue, though, that Brian Callahan doesn't end up a loser. He divorces a wife who he felt was holding him back, and now he's free to pursue whatever he pleases. But Brian is so shallow to begin with that there really aren't any depths for him to sink to. He changes little, since he already has what he wants.

Chip is the only seeming exception to this laundry list of losing men, this may be because at the beginning of the novel Chip has really bottomed out—it's not clear he can go much lower. He's just come out of one of the most humiliating situations imaginable, and he has no money, no job, and no girlfriend. Having him lose any more would not only be cruel, but might strain the novel's credibility as well.

"CHIP COMES OUT AHEAD BY REINVENTING THE AMERICAN DREAM."

The Corrections is about the loss of the American dream. It's a story about a family that has lived past those idyllic times of the suburban 1950s and 1960s when everything seemed possible. The children are now grown, fending for themselves, and the parents are retired, living on a pension. It's like the hangover the day after the party. The consequences of the excessive optimism have to be faced, and nobody except Chip seems up to the task.

Gary fails at recreating the American dream with his family. Even though he has the house, the job, and the wife and kids, he has to sacrifice his sense of self just to keep up appearances. The result is that Gary's life is a false American dream. If we look beyond the façade of Gary's perfect home in the perfect neighborhood, we find someone who is dead inside.

Denise rejects this model of how life must be lived. Instead, she moves into a life that is anti–American dream—in fact, she even becomes a source of the destruction of the American dream. First, she sleeps with several married men and then violates the model even more dramatically by sleeping with a married woman. In a sense, lesbianism—or homosexuality in general—is the antithesis of the traditional American dream, in which the husband goes off to work and the wife stays at home taking care of the kids.

By the end of the novel, Enid has also given up the American dream and its straightjacket of expectations. Her husband is off in a nursing home, and she now lives alone. For the first time in her life, she discovers a happiness free of anxiety. It's clear that this life suits Enid, even though it's outside the traditional idea of the idyllic American family. But Alfred doesn't find the kind of peace Enid has. He degenerates further into his illness until he no longer responds to anything beyond his hallucinations. In a sense, Alfred has traveled to a reality beyond the American dream.

Chip is the only one who revises the American dream into a healthier and more positive form. By the end of the novel, he has abandoned a lifestyle—or maybe the lifestyle has abandoned him—that ran counter to the American dream. He returns home to the Midwest to be the dutiful son. Chip selflessly cares for his father—which Franzen portrays as the right thing to do—and is rewarded by meeting his future wife, who happens to be Alfred's neurologist. She and Chip move in together, she becomes pregnant, and they marry. Essentially, they settle into a traditional American life, with one small modification—Chip stays at home with the baby while his wife brings home the bacon. Chip is also free to work on his screenplay. In this way, Chip's new life achieves an American dream, but one that is a slightly different variety.

"NOBODY WINS—THEY ALL HAVE LOUSY LIVES, EVEN AT THE END."

Alfred and Gary are the most obvious losers in the family. Alfred has lost contact with reality and is on a downward slope to death. Gary seems to be repeating the sins of his father by shutting down his interior life to adapt to his wife. The consequences of Gary's choice clearly aren't uplifting. Gary has a pretty miserable life that's only occasionally distracted by sensory pleasures like sex, vacations, and toys.

Denise might appear to be better off than Alfred and Gary, but when has work ever been completely fulfilling? We see that it isn't for Denise. If it were, she wouldn't have gotten involved in so many disastrous relationships because she wouldn't have needed them. Sex and other relationships outside of the kitchen merely would have been slight diversions, not all-consuming encounters. At the end of the novel, Denise is left with work, which can't completely satisfy her. And even though she's clearly aware that involvement with married men (or women) is a bad idea, it doesn't seem as if she's really learned anything from her previous disastrous relationship. We end the novel feeling that we can expect more of the same from Denise, which isn't too promising.

Enid might seem to be happy on the surface, but the only way she's been able to find peace is to be left alone in an empty house. A life where the only significant interaction is with members of a bridge club isn't much of a life—it's pretty empty, bound to be filled with superficial diversions like watching TV. This kind of life isn't much to recommend. If Enid had some sort of overriding interests, passions, goals, or hobbies, then her solitude might be something to admire—but she doesn't, as Franzen admits. Enid just drifts along in a daily routine with little to offer.

Then there's Chip. Throughout most of the novel, his life is a shambles. He is been fired from his job. His screenplay is terrible. He's in terrible debt. He's living in a sublet apartment, but a sublet. He has stooped to scamming unsuspecting investors on the Internet. He's robbed and almost killed in Lithuania. Nothing he tries on his own works out. His only recourse is to fall back on the default model that he learned in childhood—the traditional, cookie-cutter suburban family. This choice is conventional and unimaginative. It rings of defeat rather than triumph. Chip tried to create a new model, a new pattern for himself, but he failed. In the end, we feel as if Chip's acceptance of a lifestyle that he hated for so long just condemns him to repeat his parents' mistakes.

○ ○ ○

Is the world of *The Corrections* an accurate representation of American life?

"YES—FRANZEN HITS THE NAIL ON THE HEAD."

In a letter to the Russian writer Ivan Turgenev, the French novelist Gustave Flaubert admitted, "[R]eality, as I see it, should be a springboard." In *The Corrections,* Franzen accurately represents America in the 1990s—a decade of the quick fix defined by greed, envy, resentment, acquisitiveness, and self-delusion. Franzen pulls off this feat by taking a few cultural stereotypes of the 1990s and exploring them, almost to the level of caricature.

In the 1990s, biotechnology made dramatic leaps that changed the way we think of and treat illness. One example is the rise of seratonin uptake inhibitors like Prozac. At the end of the 1980s, these kinds of antidepressants were hardly a blip on the horizon, but by the end of the

1990s they were some of the biggest money-makers for pharmaceutical companies. Franzen tracks this rise of the "miracle" drugs with the subplot including Axon, the biotech startup. *The Corrections* includes not only Axon's proposed miracle drug for Parkinson's and Alzheimer's, but also the Ecstasy-like Aslan and the party drug Mexican A. The miracle of pharmaceuticals seems boundless. Franzen also shows the financial side of this miracle-drug phenomenon, as Gary gets drawn into the irrational giddiness of Axon's IPO offer and loses his shirt.

Another phenomenon of the 1990s was the celebrity chef. Maybe the most prominent is Martha Stewart, who parlayed a catering business into a multinational empire. On less superhuman levels, America saw chef celebrities like Emeril Lagasse and Paul Prudhomme, who together practically wiped out the population of red fish in Louisiana. In *The Corrections*, Denise embodies the times in her success as chef at the Generator. Franzen infuses Denise with the quirkiness and self-absorbed nature we've seen in celebrity chefs on TV. She isn't content with general glowing praise, but obsesses on reviewers' responses to her sauerkraut. When the restaurant's manager doesn't seem to appreciate her sauerkraut fully, she fires him, believing that his lack of enthusiasm is the reason her pickled cabbage isn't all the rage.

"NO—IT'S TOO ABSURD TO TAKE SERIOUSLY."

A novel that features a character that hooks up with a Lithuanian official turned mobster to bilk investors out of thousands of dollars through an Internet site can hardly be considered anything but a farce. This whole plot digression into eastern Europe pushes the bounds of believability. Franzen goes over the top with details like a city built of radioactive cinderblocks from Belarus. He piles it on with Alfred's hallucinations of attacking turds, Enid's coupon-clipping obsessive-compulsiveness, and Denise's bizarre and incessant impulse to mix her sex life with her professional life. The only Lambert who seems remotely anchored in reality is Gary—but that's only because he appears to have a stereotypical life, with a wife and kids, a good job, a nice house, and disposable income.

But isn't Gary's existence a fantasy too? Aren't most Americans living from paycheck to paycheck? Gary's reality only represents the top one percent of Americans, which to the rest of the country might as well be fantasy. Gary's world ends up coming across as a kind of "lifestyles of the rich and famous." The world of *The Corrections* is so highly distilled and exaggerated that it can't stand in for the real world. As a result, it's tough to identify with the characters. We can only be entertained, not transformed.

○   ○   ○

Why does Franzen focus so much attention on drugs — Mexican A, Aslan, Corecktall?

"HE JUST WANTS TO MOCK OUR MEDICATED CULTURE AND ALL THE GREED AND HYPE OF THE PHARMACEUTICAL INDUSTRY."

In the last decade, pharmaceutical companies have become far more prominent in popular culture than they used to be. Their ads are everywhere, programming us to look to prescriptions rather than inside ourselves for answers. *The Corrections* shows Franzen's disgust for our self-medicated culture and the greedy pharmaceutical companies that sell this idea to us every day. Franzen's exasperation comes through clearly during the lunch at Chip's apartment, when Denise snaps angrily at Enid's complaints about caring for Alfred: "So drug him and forget him. A convenient theory."

Franzen also takes jabs at the pharmaceutical culture when describing Chip's drug holiday with Melissa, who feeds Chip pill after pill of Mexican A while they hole up in a motel. When Chip takes the drug, he's essentially taken out of time, completely forgetting about the disasters in his life. He's in a terrible spot — when the dean of the college has a stroke and retires, Chip's only powerful ally for tenure is gone. He knows that as a white male he now has no chance against the politically correct minority, female candidate. The weekend of sex and Mexican A seems like a quick fix. But when Chip returns, he's forced to deal with reality — the consequences of his new tenure disadvantage and of his drug-crazed fling too.

Franzen's most serious look at the legal drug culture involves Enid and Aslan. Chip uses Mexican A just for a weekend romp, but Enid thinks Aslan might change her whole life. The drug seems like a wonderful opportunity for the truly miserable, and Enid definitely fits into that category. At first, she embraces the drug, and life seems great. But when the second shipment of Aslan arrives via her neighbor, Enid has an ethical crisis and decides to flush the pills down the drain instead.

Behind the push for self-medication are the big pharmaceutical businesses, who, Franzen indicates are far more concerned with profit than with the ethical aspects of their drugs. The main medical subplot in *The Corrections* isn't about healing but about greed. The real story with Corecktall isn't what it could do for Alzheimer's and Parkinson's sufferers but how much profit it could mean to investors. Franzen's portrayal of the IPO presentation in the hotel conference room is a great satire. Denise is the only person in the room who cares about Corecktall's effectiveness in treating mental illness—the others all just see dollar signs, salivating over the Axon presentation like hungry wolves. Franzen uses Denise to let us know just how much this behavior appalls him.

Franzen's take on the biotech industry is dead-on, especially when we look at it with hindsight. Looking through lens of a bearish stock market, we see how foolish the inflated IPO rhetoric was. We read with a cynicism we didn't have before we saw celebrities start going on the *Today* show to endorse prescription drugs.

At the end of the novel, we're left with the idea that there really isn't much difference between street drugs and prescription drugs. In a sense, pharmaceutical companies and street pushers are in the same business—selling drugs without concern for the consumer. The only thing protecting us from these corporations is the government. The only reason Enid can't get Aslan in America is the FDA and its regulations. Franzen compares the American drug market, which has laws protecting consumers, with the more open European market to illustrate the dangers of a prescription-drug market without oversight. In Europe, Enid can score Aslan with only mild caution from a doctor. For Franzen, pharmaceutical conglomerates are the real evildoers, and the government and consumers need to hold them in check.

"FRANZEN REALLY DOES SOMETHING NEW BY LOOKING AT THE CHEMICAL SIDES OF MOOD AND PERSONALITY."

Any decent author could satirize our medicated culture and profit-hungry drug companies—they're easy targets. *The Corrections* is brilliant because Franzen takes things a step further. He's one of the first major novelists to consider the brain-chemistry side of our emotions without dismissing it entirely. Up to this point, most writers have asked questions about whether emotions are inborn, influenced by society, or affected by big events in a person's life. But here, we see characters like Chip, Gary, and Enid confront the fact that at least some portion of their mental states is governed by biochemistry—a factor they don't have any control over.

When Chip hits rock bottom after losing both Melissa and his teaching job, he gets stuck in a biochemical rut. He sits in his apartment woefully aware that there's not much he can do about his mood: "[H]is endorphins had gone home to the four corners of his brain like war-weary troops. . . . [N]othing, except possibly Melissa in the flesh, could marshal them again." This passage isn't only hilarious, but pathetically true—at this point, Chip is probably a prime candidate for antidepressants.

When we meet Gary, he's obsessed with endorphins too. He's annoyed to have to take responsibility for "his own personal brain chemistry." For the first time in several weeks, he's finally in a good mood. But he doesn't just attribute it to positive changes in his life—he says it's due to the fact that "his levels of Neurofactor 3 . . . were posting seven-day or even thirty-day highs, that his Factor 2 and Factor 7 levels were likewise outperforming expectations." Gary's happy for some reason, and he likes to think it's because his own biochemical stock market is bullish. He feels comfortable because he can blame his good or bad moods on chemical indices that he has about as much control over as he has over the Nasdaq.

Enid faces biochemical issues head-on when she talks to the doctor on the cruise ship. This is where the ethical issues get deep. The doctor promises that Aslan will shut off all of Enid's shame, worry, and other so-called bad emotions. Enid realizes it's probably true that some of her irrational feelings of shame are biochemical, but she still wonders whether it's good to shut down these feelings. They seem to be a big part of her personality—the things that make her Enid. Eventually, she reaches the conclusion that Aslan is bad, that she can work through her problems without the aid of personality-altering drugs.

In this sense, *The Corrections* recalls an earlier book, Peter Kramer's *Listening to Prozac* (1993). Kramer raises the concern of whether it's right to make people feel better artificially. He asks whether Prozac and other drugs that limit a person's feelings actually inhibit a person's self-hood and his or her ability to grow through suffering. Franzen has the same concern with Aslan, and he ups the ante even more with Corecktall. The drug supposedly not only reverses Parkinson's, but has the potential to empty prisons by correcting criminal behavior—hence the name. This drug is so powerful that it could change people's basic natures. Franzen doesn't believe such a drug can ever exist—or even if it did, that it should. Yes, brain chemistry plays a part in our emotions—and Franzen's one of the first writers to explore that—but that doesn't mean we can just start taking pills that fundamentally alter our personalities and selves.

○ ○ ○

Chip's section contains references to two famous twentieth-century cultural critics— Walter Benjamin and Michel Foucault. Why does Franzen include them?

"FRANZEN JUST WANTS TO SHOW HOW SUPERFICIAL THE ACADEMIC WORLD IS."

Franzen is a pro at capturing the environment of intense insecurity that exists in college English departments. These departments are full of people who have spent eight or nine years (or more) of study to earn a doctorate in a field that has less and less influence on contemporary culture with each passing day. Few look to literature anymore to interpret contemporary times when they're inundated with nonstop streaming news from hundreds of different sources—satellite TV, the Internet, newspapers, magazines, radio stations. The value of literature has plummeted. Literary academics see their work becoming more obsolete each day and struggle to reinvigorate their field with meaning.

The blockbuster novel has redefined literature as entertainment. Serious literature is simply no longer read on the scale it once was. There are much easier, more accurate, and perhaps more essential venues for gaining knowledge. In a world that values material products of hard work, discussions about truth in *Hamlet* don't have much currency. Scholars know this, but at the same time they experience the power of good literature. This conflict fuels their insecurity. Emotionally, they know that these literary works of art are vital in intangible ways, but they feel helpless as they see popular respect for literature diminish. To compensate, English professors try to rename themselves with fancier, more stylish titles. Chip doesn't have a doctorate in English, but in "textual artifacts"—a term that suggests a weight and importance that the title "English professor" has lost.

The name-dropping is just another symptom of this desperation. Interestingly, it's not the professor but the students who mention Walter Benjamin and Michel Foucault—two pillars of twentieth-century cultural studies. Maybe more than anyone else at a college or university, students are finely tuned in to what is cutting edge. Mentioning Benjamin and Foucault in a paper or conversation is like an instant passport to the hallowed community of intellectuals. In both cases, the students seem more concerned with the name-dropping than what those men's ideas actually mean to the discussion.

"FRANZEN USES THE REFERENCES TO CLUE US IN TO THE BIGGER CULTURAL ISSUES THAT RUN THROUGH THE NOVEL."

When Franzen mentions Benjamin and Foucault, he's telling us that *The Corrections* is meant to offer striking insights and unexpected perspectives into contemporary culture, just as these two cultural theorists did. Franzen makes reference to one of Benjamin's core ideas—that to understand culture, we should look not at mainstream culture but at the refuse and debris that's shuffled aside.

The Corrections

Franzen twists this idea by implying that the marginalized culture of today is white suburban America. In his essay "Perchance to Dream," he writes that "much of contemporary fiction's vitality now resides in the black, Hispanic, Asian, Native American, gay, and women's communities, which have moved into the structures left behind by the departing straight white male." In this kind of literary environment, suburbia and its values have been shoved off center stage. *The Corrections* explores this newly ignored territory of white suburban America.

Franzen's perspective is new because for decades most people have assumed that "marginal cultures" meant racial and ethnic minorities, women, gays, and so on. Foucault was one of the first to study gay and outsider cultures in order to comment on mainstream culture. Franzen now celebrates the exact opposite of what Foucault explored forty years ago. Franzen isn't saying that Foucault's approach to analyzing the world is wrong, but that our perspective of what's mainstream and what's marginal has to change. Multiculturalism has won the day, leaving white mainstream America somewhat silenced. Franzen's goal in *The Corrections* is to bring voice back to this community.

To accomplish this, Franzen follows Benjamin's lead in exploring the marginal. Benjamin was one of the first to recognize the lure of suburban kitsch. In an unfinished book called *The Arcades Project*, he explored the Parisian glass-covered indoor arcades that were early prototypes of the modern shopping mall. Franzen picks up where Benjamin left off. He addresses the wider suburban phenomenon of mall culture. He shows us characters from a white culture that's been marginalized by today's celebration of difference. He leads us through a degenerate world that places value in material goods. This world is populated by people who don't have the faintest higher ambitions or spiritual aspirations.

Chip is more interested in getting tenure than in literature. Denise is obsessed with reviews of her restaurant. Gary desperately wants to make a killing in the stock market. Enid craves social status. The only character who seems oblivious to it all is Alfred—who has lost his mind. Curiously, Alfred is also the only character who at one time pursued what might be called higher knowledge. Years earlier, he devoted his spare time to experimenting and inventing. Of all the pursuits in the novel, Alfred's science experiments seem out of place because they weren't directed toward material pleasure. But in the end, even Alfred gives up this search, retreating to his basement recliner and eventually succumbing to Parkinson's. The last glimmer of higher aspiration is gone. We're left with a picture of white suburban America as a kitschy realm of materialism and petty social competitiveness—a caricature too bizarre to be considered mainstream.

"FRANZEN'S WRONG—WHITE AMERICA IS STILL THE MAINSTREAM, THE CONVENTIONAL."

If Franzen means to say that white America is marginalized, he's wrong. White suburban culture isn't transgressive—it's the majority, even in our time of multiculturalism. The reason people are interested in lives *unlike* their own is exactly because people like Benjamin and Foucault have done their job so well. No matter how caricatured and absurd Franzen tries to make it, suburban white America is still considered the mainstream in our day and age.

Franzen never really exploits the ideas of Benjamin and Foucault. Instead, Franzen himself is hopelessly conventional. He makes Gary renounce his transgression and accept his wife's conventional point of view. He ensures that Denise conforms by eliminating lesbianism and adultery from her life. Finally, he has Chip, the most overtly unorthodox member of the family, make a complete turnaround by moving back to the Midwest, marrying, and having children. Chip renounces his intellectual and criminal behavior to conform to the lifestyle of his suburban childhood. The concern here isn't transgression, but that nothing can be learned from these transgressions. They're simply abandoned. This emptiness is the real tragedy of this novel—and a tragedy that Franzen never fully understands.

Resurrecting the Great Novel

Franzen worked his way into the heart of the American literary scene with his fiction, his essays, and his stated goal of writing the next Great American Novel.

○ ○ ○

WHILE FRANZEN IS PROBABLY BEST KNOWN for his epic media battle with Oprah Winfrey (see "A Brief History"), the Oprah debacle is only one chapter in his considerable library of achievements.

Born the youngest of three children in Western Springs, Illinois, in 1959, Franzen spent most of his youth in the St. Louis suburb of Webster Groves, Missouri—a Midwestern childhood that mirrors the family life of *The Corrections*'s Lamberts. But Franzen took a page right out his life when he made his character of Alfred Lambert a Parkinson's sufferer. While Franzen was writing the novel, his own father died of Alzheimer's disease, the symptoms of which are closely akin to Parkinson's. Franzen wrote a moving article in *The New Yorker* about his father's battle with the disease and later decided to incorporate it in his characterization of Alfred in *The Corrections*.

Franzen graduated from Swarthmore College in 1981 and continued his studies as a Fulbright Scholar at the Freie Universität in Berlin. In 1982, he married Valerie Cornell, having met her at a gathering of a college literary magazine. By 1994, however, they had separated and eventually divorced. According to Franzen, the stress of his success as a writer in contrast to her relative obscurity was too much for the relationship to sustain.

The Corrections

During this time, Franzen published two novels to wide acclaim but miniscule sales. His first novel, *The Twenty-Seventh City* (1988), was a complex thriller about urban planning set in St. Louis. It received good reviews but died a fairly quick death in bookstores. Franzen's ingeniously intricate second novel, *Strong Motion* (1992), featured earthquakes, corporate conspiracy, and family conflict. The novel tanked, however. Franzen believed that *Strong Motion* failed because it lacked an "immediately likeable character, [and had] a bad jacket and second-novel backlash."

Franzen lived a nomadic life during these writing years. For a while, he lived in the Boston suburb of Somerville, Massachusetts, where each day he wrote for eight hours, took a dinner break, and then wrote for another five. To make ends meet, he did weekend work as a research assistant tracking earthquakes for Harvard's geology department. Franzen and his wife would go out to dinner only once a year, on their anniversary. By the time *The Twenty-Seventh City* appeared, Franzen left Somerville and lived in a series of rented apartments and borrowed houses, living a few weeks or months at one place and then moving. During this period he lived in New York City, Philadelphia, Colorado Springs, Chicago, Boston, Italy, and Spain.

Franzen's profile as a writer didn't rise until 1996, when *Harper's* published his bitter, eloquent, and highly personal essay "Perchance to Dream: In an Age of Images, a Reason to Write Novels." The piece reads like an elegy to a dead art form but also offers new hope for the novel. Like old cries for the perpetuation of the monarchy—"The king is dead. Long live the king!"—Franzen seems to say that the novel is dead. TV has killed off big, socially engaged novels, and serious postmodern novels—those by Thomas Pynchon, William Gaddis, and Don DeLillo, among others—are doomed to irrelevance. But just when the novel seems to have been relegated to the dust heap of history, Franzen offers an old, forgotten novel, Paula Fox's *Desperate Characters* (1970), as a model for the future. "At the heart of my despair about the novel had been a conflict between my feeling that I should Address the Culture and Bring News to the Mainstream, and my desire to write about the things closest to me, to lose myself in my characters and locales I loved," he wrote in the essay. For Franzen, Fox did just this, and her novel became his model for how to connect the personal and the social. Franzen

The scavenger

For an astute chronicler of contemporary American society, Franzen has quite a retro streak. In an interview with *The New Yorker*, he offered a description of the tools of his trade: "I sit at an old oaken teacher's desk scavenged from NYU. I have a cushioned metal office chair that I found by the side of a road in Rockland County in 1982. I use a used 486 IBM clone that I bought for $150 through an ad at the gym. My software is the excellent, vintage WordPerfect version 5.0, pirated long ago. I have a dot-matrix Panasonic printer, bought in 1989." One can only hope that the proceeds from *The Corrections* will pay for a licensed copy of WordPerfect, or, at the very least, a quick trip to Ikea.

aspired to create a new kind of social engagement—and his essay also raised expectations for his next novel.

The buzz from the *Harper's* essay made it possible for Franzen to sell *The Corrections* to the publishing firm Farrar, Straus & Giroux in 1996 on the basis of just 200 pages. However, by the time the novel was due a year later, Franzen had axed all but twenty pages of that initial manuscript. In the end, it took him seven years to write the novel. In between, he won numerous awards for his fiction, including a Whiting Writer's Award in 1998 and the American Academy's Berlin Prize in 2000. *The New Yorker* named Franzen one of its "Twenty Writers for the 21st Century," and *Granta* called him one of the "Best Young American Novelists." By the time the novel was finished, Franzen had sold the motion picture rights to *The Corrections* to producer Scott Rudin (who adapted Michael Chabon's *Wonder Boys* in 2000 and Michael Cunningham's *The Hours* in 2002) for six figures.

The story of Franzen's process for writing the novel has become part of literary lore. He rented a corner of a friend's Harlem studio and outfitted it with soundproof walls and a window of double-paned glass. He kept the blinds closed and the lights off in order to rid his environment of all distractions. Often, he blindfolded himself and donned earplugs and earmuffs to shut out the city's noise even further. Nevertheless, Franzen's progress went in fits and starts, with many days wasted on naps, unessential chores, and other distractions. Finally, the book began to flow, and he was able to write the majority of it in 2000, knocking off around five pages a day near the end.

The Corrections

The Corrections made a splash when it hit bookstores in early September 2001. Franzen was mentioned on the cover of a number of major American magazines, including *Vanity Fair, Esquire, The New York Times Magazine,* and *The New York Times Book Review,* among others. Reviewers acclaimed the novel as an important work. And Franzen's dustup with Oprah guaranteed that the novel wouldn't be forgotten after the terrorist attacks of September 11, 2001. *The Corrections* was nominated for every major award, including the Pulitzer Prize, the PEN/Faulkner Award, and the National Book Critics Circle Award, and it won the National Book Award. With the sales of the novel and the Hollywood screenplay deal, it's a safe bet that Franzen now could go out to dinner every night of the week and pick up his friends' checks as well.

Keeping Up With the Lamberts

From St. Jude to Manhattan, Lithuania to a cruise ship, Franzen's characters can't escape the great American rat race.

○ ○ ○

ST. JUDE IS THE CENTER of the novel—the Midwestern suburb to which everyone returns, the sun around which everything else orbits. The three younger Lamberts venture out into the larger, more complex universe but are expected to return home. St. Jude isn't any more remarkable than the thousands of other suburban developments that sprung up around urban centers after World War II. The center in these kinds of developments is the home, not the community. Each house is supposed to represent the owners' little patch of heaven. Unfortunately, the Lambert's heaven has gone to seed.

Like many of these developments planned out fifty years ago, St. Jude is beginning to show its age. Most people are more than sixty years old and retired. The lively sounds of children playing in the streets and backyards are long gone. Also gone is the unbridled postwar optimism that life will keep getting better simply because of good old American know-how. That 1950s can-do attitude—so wonderfully embodied in publications like *Popular Mechanics*—has been replaced with a strange and oddly anxious desperation. The feeling in St. Jude is one of somebody well aware that he's fighting a losing battle.

The quiet on the streets of St. Jude seems out of place. It has the eerie quality of a cemetery. It's a culture that is dying. The children who have grown up and moved away return regularly to pay their respects, just as they would to a grave. Franzen likens St. Jude to a retirement community, but the feeling of the place is even more despairing than that. The streets are empty and quiet except for the occasional passing sedan. Time has silenced the music of bouncing balls and children's laughter.

To show a contrast to St. Jude, Franzen takes us on a tour of some of America's centers of culture and commerce, with a small diversion into eastern Europe for a sampling of unfettered capitalism. These other settings are somewhat menacing in comparison to the benign blandness of St. Jude. "The Failure" takes place in New York City, with a short flashback to a New England college campus. We encounter the Big Apple in a driving rainstorm. To emphasize the city's difference from nice and placid St. Jude, Franzen places his characters on Ninth Street in Greenwich Village. Though it's not the center of hip culture—that's further downtown in Tribeca, at least for the moment—the Village still has a bohemian atmosphere that the influx of yuppies and Gap stores can't scrape away completely. A cultural awareness exists in places like the Cedar Tavern, where the New York School of poets and abstract expressionists drank in the 1950s and 1960s. This is the watering hole where Chip steals money off the bar.

From this Manhattan scene, we're transported back to a New England college campus where Chip toiled as an assistant professor before his termination for dallying with a student. Franzen beautifully characterizes the paradoxes of this world of seemingly higher learning. Junior faculty members are paid so little that they're forced to live in college-subsidized housing on the edge of an ecological disaster area. On the surface, campus life has the appearance of tranquility, but underneath is an environment where the powerful toy with the insecurities of the powerless. Chip's affair with Melissa is small potatoes compared to the battle of favor-currying he has to fight to win tenure. In some ways the rat race for tenure is like the backstage of a

> On the surface, campus life has the appearance of tranquility, but underneath is an environment where the powerful toy with the insecurities of the powerless.

Miss America competition. It doesn't always matter who's the prettiest or the most talented—it's about who makes the right connections.

In the next book, we jump from the city to the more rarified enclaves of northwest Philadelphia and the city's downtown industrial areas. Northwest Philadelphia is the old, moneyed section of the city. It is predominantly white and features grand homes of half a million dollars or more. There's an aura of elegance and sophistication from a bygone era, a sense of privilege and inevitability that life will unfold in predictable and secure ways. Gary has settled in this community with his rich wife. Since Gary himself wasn't born into wealth, he's somewhat insecure about deserving this elite life, which contrasts with his wife's attitude. We can see this contrast played out in Gary and Caroline's children. The sons seem at home in their environment. They have an attitude of entitlement that comes from getting what they want when they want it. Part of Gary's problem is that he hasn't found a comfort zone in northwest Philadelphia.

Next is Enid and Alfred's cruise ship, a microenvironment similar to St. Jude in that it's completely separated from the rest of the world. As in a suburb, everyone on the cruise ship is on the same level. The social and economic hierarchies that separate people in the real world are stripped away on a cruise ship. Enid and Alfred sit at the dinner table with the rich and the educated without any worries that their middle-class roots are an issue. Enid even swaps intimacies with a rich doctor's wife. They also attend a seminar on investment together as if their concerns were the same. The cruise ship offers a utopia where everyone is on equal footing.

This utopian society stands in sharp contrast to the hyper-competitive setting of Denise's high-end culinary world. In the world of expensive big-city restaurants, the Generator exists only to earn a five-star rating. The personal satisfaction of kitchen employees isn't a consideration. Denise thrives so much in this competitive environment that even a great review isn't enough. She wants the food critics to love something in particular—her sauerkraut. Nothing short of complete and total success is of any value. Personal growth and feelings have no place here.

The post-Soviet free-for-all of Vilnius, Lithuania, has the same Darwinian quality. It's survival of the fittest in an economy with few controls and where it's possible to pay off anyone in the government. The weak will be destroyed. Chip does well in this setting as long as he has a powerful protector. The moment someone else muscles his way into power,

The Corrections

Chip's life and status lose value. He's simply prey to be fleeced, and he's lucky to get out of eastern Europe in a plane rather than a pine box.

What's strange in *The Corrections* is that all the Lamberts return to the idyll of St. Jude, where overaggressive ambition is just not acceptable and where social climbing is frowned upon. It's a world where Enid and Alfred can be invited to a housewarming at the home of the richest couple in town. What are we to make of this return? Franzen clearly tries to contrast St. Jude with the outside world, but it's not clear if he values one over the other. In the end, neither world seems particularly appealing.

The Oprah Wars

The Corrections brought Franzen fame and fortune—and a ten-round grudge match with the most powerful woman in media.

○   ○   ○

JONATHAN FRANZEN COULD GO DOWN in literary history as the man who snubbed Oprah. Though he may not have played any part in Oprah Winfrey's decision to end the Oprah Book Club, his derogatory remarks about her show and her fans caused a hell of a stir.

The affair began in late September 2001, when Oprah announced *The Corrections* as one of her book club selections. The Oprah stamp of approval was every publisher's dream, a seeming guarantee of a million copies sold. In their rush to make sales, lucky Oprah-favored publishers promptly slapped a sticker on the cover of each copy of their book, broadcasting the selection.

A slight problem arose, though, when Franzen's response to the Oprah pick wasn't particularly gracious. Rather than gush with thanks like most previous Oprah honorees, Franzen objected to the idea of his publisher stamping the Oprah emblem on the cover of his novel. He winced at the thought of someone smacking a corporate logo on "my creation." Franzen then labeled some of Oprah's previous book selections "schmaltzy" and "one-dimensional" while he characterizing himself as a writer "solidly in the high-art literary tradition."

Quickly realizing he had opened a Pandora's box, Franzen followed his criticisms with some desperate, ham-handed comments about Oprah being "really smart" and "fighting the good fight." But try as he might,

The Corrections

Franzen simply couldn't dig himself out of the hole he had created. Oprah promptly disinvited him from the book-club segment on her show: "Jonathan Franzen will not be on the Oprah Winfrey show because he is seemingly uncomfortable and conflicted about being chosen as a book club selection," Oprah announced. "It is never my intention to make anyone uncomfortable or cause anyone conflict."

The Oprah storm aside, the reception that greeted *The Corrections* was a writer's dream come true. Whereas critics and readers all but ignored Franzen's first two novels, this third novel had a prepublication buzz that guaranteed bookstores would display it prominently. The tremendous publicity also made it possible for Franzen to sell the novel's motion-picture rights for a tidy sum.

Within days of its publication in September 2001, *The Corrections* was treated to rapturous reviews in seemingly every major publication—the *Atlantic Monthly, The New York Times Book Review,* the *Christian Science Monitor, USA Today, The New Republic, O the Oprah Magazine, Entertainment Weekly,* and *The New York Review of Books,* among many others. Mentions of Franzen were splashed on the covers of the *New York Times Magazine, Vanity Fair,* and *Esquire,* and interviews appeared in publications all over the country. Oprah's selection of *The Corrections* vir-

A way with words

Even more alarming than Franzen's anti-Oprah tirades were his astonishingly feeble attempts at damage control afterward. In seemingly every interview he gave in the months following the Oprah debacle, Franzen planted his foot firmly in his mouth, leaving a trail of PR disasters in his wake. In an interview with *USA Today,* Franzen said he felt "awful" for dissing Oprah, for "giving offense to someone who's a hero—not a hero of mine per se, but a hero in general—I feel bad." Oprah, mercifully, didn't respond. Then, in an interview with *The Independent* in January 2002, Franzen not only graciously validated Oprah's selection of his novel—"In fact, *The Corrections* was a good Oprah choice because I have low taste myself"—but also placed himself high on the list of dangers to American society: "We had op-ed pages in the *New York Times* where it was Anthrax, Anthrax, Afghanistan, Afghanistan, and the Villain Franzen."

tually guaranteed blockbuster sales. The book had hit every major best-seller list by the second week it was on the shelves.

Fortune heralded it as the "novel of the year" and the *Atlantic Monthly* called it a masterpiece comparable to John Cheever's *The Wapshot Chronicles. The New York Times Book Review* claimed that Franzen was a master of wordplay on the level of Vladimir Nabokov and said that *The Corrections* has "everything we want in a novel." The professional writers' publication *Poets & Writers* described the "sweeping scope and the sympathy of its tone" as comparable to the works of Leo Tolstoy and Thomas Pynchon. Other reviewers saw echoes of David Foster Wallace's *Infinite Jest* and Don DeLillo's *Underworld*—two works whose authors are friends of Franzen's. The *New York Observer* lauded Franzen's ability "to risk sentimentality to get at emotional truth." As a whole, reviewers recognized the importance of Franzen's novel and placed him with other great writers.

In particular, David Gates in the *New York Times Book Review* marveled at the extraordinary breadth and scope of *The Corrections.* Gates wrote that the novel captivates the reader's attention so completely that other books are forgotten—it "creates the illusion of giving a complete account of a world." But Gates criticizes the beginning of *The Corrections* for having the same kind of "hump" for the reader to get over that Chip has in his screenplay. Nevertheless, Gates feels the novel is so good that the "hump" is worth the work.

USA Today's Bob Minzesheimer praised Franzen's ability to capture American culture at the turn of the millennium, admiring the "dead-on portrayal of a culture that's obsessed with material success and clings to the promise of new technology and a quick fix for all that ails us." Minzesheimer also enjoyed the ending's redemptive quality, which he found a surprise. He wrote that the ending of *The Corrections* speaks to all of us in respect to our desire to change things for the better.

Other acclaimed American novelists also stepped forward to declare *The Corrections* an important work of literature. Don DeLillo praised the work as "powerful." David Foster Wallace called it "a testament to the range and depth of pleasures of great fiction." Michael Cunningham applauded the novel's complexity, "its grasp of the subtle relationship between domestic drama and global events." Pat Conroy marveled at Franzen's ambition and heralded him as one of the brightest new authors

The Corrections

on the horizon. Francine Prose was awed by the way *The Corrections* "revealed so accurately, so transparently—and finally, so forgivingly" the Lamberts' lives and their struggles to find happiness. Perhaps this is why *Time* magazine asserted that the novel would become "that rare thing, a literary work that everybody's reading."

The Corrections is perhaps the first novel since Tom Wolfe's *The Bonfire of the Vanities* (1987) to generate such buzz. Franzen's novel is the big book that readers and reviewers have been dreaming of. From the small details and descriptions to the wide sweep of the narrative, the breadth of Franzen's work has astonished virtually everyone. It's no wonder the book has been so successful.

The question now is whether Franzen can follow *The Corrections* with a similar success. He may have to deal with lingering bad publicity, the vestiges of the uproar he created when he criticized the Oprah Book Club as a middlebrow institution. This comment brought intense criticism from the publishing industry and from America as a whole. Nobody likes an ungrateful elitist, and that's how Franzen came across. Although he tried to retract his comments, they're not easily forgettable or forgivable. But regardless of the fact that Franzen has weathered quite a lot of disdain, the Oprah fiasco sent sales of *The Corrections* through the roof. Now it's just a question of whether Franzen's next novel can ride that same wave of notoriety.

Other Books of Interest

In writing *The Corrections* and his earlier novels, Franzen has turned to a number of American literary giants for inspiration.

○ ○ ○

BY JONATHAN FRANZEN

THE TWENTY-SEVENTH CITY
(Farrar, Straus & Giroux, 1988)

The Twenty-Seventh City is Franzen's first novel. It's set in St. Louis, Missouri, and centers on the plight of this dying Midwestern city: the corruption, ambition, power, money, and apathy. The spark that ignites the trouble in the novel is the hiring of the city's new police chief, a charismatic young woman from Bombay, India. A classic all-encompassing political conspiracy erupts that turns the city inside out. This is a suspense novel that transcends the genre.

STRONG MOTION
(Farrar, Straus & Giroux, 1992)

Franzen's second novel follows a man named Louis Holland, who arrives in Boston one spring when earthquakes strike the city. His grandmother dies in the first earthquake, and Louis gets embroiled in a complicated and nasty battle over her will. In the middle of this fight, he meets and falls in love with Renée Seitchek, a seismologist who discovers the origins of the earthquakes. The complications that arise are almost enough to ruin Louis. The novel contains many of the characteristic traits of Franzen's work—the combination of domestic and global themes, stunning detail, social commentary, and morality.

The Corrections

"PERCHANCE TO DREAM: IN THE AGE OF IMAGES, A REASON TO WRITE NOVELS"
(*Harper's*, April 1996)

This essay is Franzen's aesthetic manifesto. He discusses the purpose of good fiction, the unique personality traits of readers and writers, how good novels address both internal and societal issues, and more. Taking its title from a soliloquy by Hamlet, "Perchance to Dream" lays out the ideas about fiction that Franzen puts into play in *The Corrections*.

"MY FATHER'S BRAIN"
(*The New Yorker*, September 10, 2001)

Published the week *The Corrections* hit bookstores and a week before the September 11 terrorist attacks, this thoughtful, caring essay recounts Franzen's memories of his father's decline due to Alzheimer's disease. The article provides insight into Franzen's development of the character of Alfred Lambert in *The Corrections*. This window in the author's life also suggests that the novel is not completely invented, but has been inspired by his own life and family.

BY OTHER AUTHORS

DESPERATE CHARACTERS
by Paula Fox (W.W. Norton & Company, 1970)

Fox's novel addresses the social and personal in a way that changed Franzen's understanding of fiction, and formed the basis of his famous *Harper's* essay "Perchance to Dream." *Desperate Characters* follows Sophie, a literate Brooklynite who is married to a conservative lawyer. One day, a stray cat bites Sophie while she's feeding it. The bite and her subsequent healing become symbolic of her desire to ignore the horrible social realities around her—from the Vietnam War to the derelicts on the street.

UNDERWORLD
by Don DeLillo (Scribner, 1997)

Don DeLillo has had more influence on Franzen work than any other writer, having been his mentor over the years. While writing *The Corrections*, Franzen read the manuscript for *Underworld*, and he has stated that the work profoundly influenced him. *Underworld* is a dark, expansive novel that offers a panoramic vision of America over the past half century.

INFINITE JEST
by David Foster Wallace (Little, Brown, 1996)

At roughly 1,000 pages, *Infinite Jest* is a gargantuan novel. Wallace is one of Franzen's closest writing friends. The two are critical darlings, having been named part of *Time* magazine's "Fiction's New Fab Four" (along with Rick Moody and Donald Antrim) and *The New Yorker*'s "Twenty Writers for the 21st Century." *Infinite Jest* is set in a postmillennial America that's depressing, toxic, and totally commercialized. Set partly at an alcoholics' halfway house and partly at a competitive tennis school, the novel is so wide-ranging that it's virtually impossible to summarize.

"WRITING AMERICAN FICTION"
by Philip Roth (*Commentary*, March 1961; September 1961)

Roth's famous essay on fiction argues that the big social novel is dead. He convincingly points out that these kinds of stories can't compete with the real-life news that people find every night on television. In many ways, Franzen's essay "Perchance to Dream" and his novel *The Corrections* are attempts to reinvigorate the social novel with the power and meaning that Roth said it could no longer contain.

"STALKING THE BILLION-FOOTED BEAST"
by Tom Wolfe (*Harper's*, November 1989)

After the huge success of his novel *Bonfire of the Vanities* (1987), Wolfe tried to set out in words what he thought the great American novel should do. He argues for the revival of the sweeping, realistic novel of the nineteenth century. In his view, novels need to address big issues, not small, domestic ones. If novels don't turn to realism based on sound reporting, journalists will capture the high ground of literature. Though Franzen doesn't make quite the same argument, both authors agree that today's novels must address larger cultural issues.

LISTENING TO PROZAC
by Peter D. Kramer (Viking Press, 1993)

This fascinating nonfiction book examines how the rise of so-called miracle drugs like Prozac have affected the way our culture looks for quick fixes. Kramer tackles the moral and philosophical issues regarding the use of medication to improve one's life—the same issues that come up in

The Corrections

The Corrections. What is the nature of human character? What accounts for disturbances of that character? Is human personality shaped by nature or nurture? And what are the ethics of altering personality?